World Traveler Press
Colorado USA
www.WorldTravelerPress.com

Cover design by Sanja Spajić

Chance Encounters: Travel Tales from Around the World
First edition

ISBN 978-0-0000000-0-0 (Print)
ISBN 978-0-9908786-1-2 (E-book)

"Travel is more than the seeing of sites. It is a change that goes on deep and permanent in the ideas of living."

—MIRIAM BEARD

CONTENTS

INTRODUCTION

It's almost 10:30 p.m., but the sun has spread a deep pink and orange swath across the horizon, providing plenty of light as we row toward shore. Here in Sweden, summer days are long and sweet. The Swedes relish these long days with gusto. Many head to cottages on a lake, where they can unwind, relax and recharge.

That's what I'm doing here in Sweden, too — living in a cottage on an island outside of Stockholm. True, it's only for a week or two, but it's enough time to become a pseudo-Scandinavian and savor each moment of the summer sun.

My sweetheart and I have joined in on the fun, rowing our aged boat along the forested shore. We pass a group of children splashing happily in the lake as the waters grow dark. Although I don't understand their words, their groans of disapproval are universal as their mother gathers them in for bed.

We bring the rowboat up on shore and then stretch our legs with a walk down a tree-lined lane. I can hear the crickets starting their song, and waves slapping against the sandy shore. Suddenly, a man steps out of the shadows. His appearance startles me, and I wonder if I should be afraid. But then I notice he is walking a small dog, and he greets me kindly in Swedish.

I laugh and mumble an unintelligent response. He doesn't mind and replies in English, the beginning of a wonderful conversation. It turns out that Roland is our neighbor this week on the lake. We talk of everything from home to hiking to customs to travel — two Americans and a Dutchman just shooting the breeze in the waning light of a Swedish summer sun. By the end of our chat, our new friend has invited us to go water skiing the next day, something we never expected to do here.

It's funny how such chance encounters can add depth to a journey. As we row back to the island, I know that I'll remember our time with Roland long after memories of my visits to Swedish castles and museums have faded.

Travel has a way of making the world a much smaller place. It removes us from our day-to-day routines and the well-worn paths of our lives, and takes us down unexpected roads and into uncharted waters. Often, we cross paths with those we would otherwise never meet — and those encounters can leave a mark on our lives, whether for a brief moment or a lifelong memory.

This collection of stories celebrates these encounters, from heartwarming and humorous tales of the human spirit to thought-provoking essays of a life now altered.

In the 15 years I've spent as a travel journalist, I've covered destinations all over the globe. But the stories I remember most are of the people I've met — the Kansas farmer who shared his love for the land, the wizened guide who introduced me to Aboriginal Australia and the handsome Swedish boy long ago who introduced me to this beautiful land.

Although it didn't work out with that handsome Swedish boy (sorry Mats!), I've held onto his love of Sweden. It seemed the perfect place to work on the book you now hold in your hands (or on your screen).

Along with some of my own favorite travel encounters, I've gathered stories from top travel writers around the world. I've spent the last week reading through their tales in my chair by the lake, and have learned that travel experiences that bring human lives together are important to all of us.

Kimberley Lovato's tale of an elevator ride with a courageous woman in Paris packs deep emotions into a matter of minutes, from recollections of childhood memories to profound realizations of life.

Nithin Coca's conversation with a taxi driver in the United Arab Emirates leaves an impression that he won't forget, and during a hike with a young monk in Bhutan, Shilpa Gupta learns a lesson not about Buddhism, but about herself.

Sometimes, those we meet while traveling alter our lives in profound ways. Meeting a shell-dyer in Huatulco, Mexico helps Michele Peterson reconsider her newfound fears after recovering from a bout of illness, and Rick Zullo decides it's time to move onto the next chapter of his life after an unusual day in Sicily. My own story from the former East Berlin shows how a supposed "enemy" can become a lifelong friend.

Traveling often takes us out of our comfort zone. Sometimes it puts us face-to-face with hardship and the power of the human spirit. Cece Romanyshyn is moved by the strength of three young Kenyan sisters who are faced with a heart-wrenching local custom, and Rob Woodburn marvels at the resourcefulness of two young men from Malawi in their quest for a decent pair of shoes.

Those we meet while traveling can enrich us in ways we never imagined, such as when Margie Goldsmith spent a joyous afternoon dancing and playing harmonica with a group of Batwa pygmies in Uganda, and when C. Lill Ahrens learned a unique lesson from her ever-patient landlord in Korea.

Meeting others during our travels can allow us to view life through different eyes. A golden-toothed guide in Albania gives Peter Mandel an enjoyable tour of his homeland, providing insight that he would never get from a guidebook, and a young girl named Alice gives Annia Lekka a different perspective of Nepal.

Sometimes strangers provide a helping hand when it's needed most. Sofie Couwenbergh met not one, but three different Americans who helped give her the courage to pursue her dream, and Gabriella Brand crossed paths with a couple in Japan who gave her hiking advice and then a place to stay.

These are just some of the inspiring, touching and even humorous stories in Chance Encounters. I hope these tales encourage you to set off on your own adventures — and that you'll come back with some cherished stories of your own.

Janna Graber is an American travel journalist, editor and producer who has covered travel in more than 38 countries. She fell in love with exploring other countries and cultures while studying abroad in Austria, and has been hooked ever since. She is the managing editor at GoWorldTravel.com, and has written for Parade, Reader's Digest, Outside, The Chicago Tribune and many more. Read more of her work at jannagraber.com or follow her on Twitter @AColoradoGirl.

Chance Encounters
TRAVEL TALES FROM
AROUND THE WORLD

BEGINNINGS
Paris, France

Not much bigger than a wine barrel, the hotel elevator is one of those cage-style carriages typical in ancient Parisian buildings, embellished on three sides with delicate gold swirls and flourishes, and an industrial crisscross gate for a door that collapses and expands in graceless clacks. There's a woman in the elevator with me, and even with my back pressed against the farthest edge of the enclosure, she is close enough to touch.

"Would you push number five for me?" she asks. "I'm having trouble with my hands today."

I poke the black button next to the cutout number five, then the one next to the six, my floor. The gate slams shut, and my knees plié at the jerk of the taut cables. With a steady robotic thrum the elevator begins to ascend sluggishly, as if being hand-heaved by two men in the basement.

I stare at the elevator panel for a few seconds, wanting the digits to light and extinguish more quickly, but I can't help but notice the woman's crutches. They are permanent buttresses that prop her erect and tether her thin legs and scuffed shoes to steady ground. There are no padded ledges beneath her armpits on which to rest. Instead, rigid, 4-inch cuffs lock around the black long sleeves covering her slight forearms.

A cell phone shrill makes me blink. The woman struggles as she maneuvers her hands around the zipper of a brown saddle-shaped purse slung across her chest.

"Can I help you with that?" I ask, nodding toward the purse.

"Yes, thank you," she says.

I reach over and slide the zipper open, pull out the phone and place it in her open palm.

It's her mother, I conclude, who is waiting in their room.

"She's always so worried about me now," the woman tells me when she hangs up. "I just wanted to be alone for a while."

I nod. As a mother, I empathize with the anxiety of wondering where your child is. As a daughter, I understand the desire to veer off a course that is planned for you and chart one that is meant for you, even if it's just to wander for an hour through narrow French streets.

*****

Two decades earlier, I'd taken my first trip to Paris for reasons spawned by quixotic stories and a poster of the Eiffel Tower I'd pinned to the closet door of my bedroom in second grade. But arriving in France, for me, was more than just a trip. It was proof that it was possible to *live* a life instead of *wish* it.

For years I'd listened to my mother dream aloud of going to Hawaii, Maine, Greece and other far-flung places. When the foggy June mornings arrived in our southern California neighborhood each year, she'd tell me it was her favorite time to be at the beach. But she never went. Not to Hawaii, or Maine, or Greece. Her wishes were checked behind excuses of limited time and money, traffic and other self-imposed hurdles. "Maybe someday," was her shrug-of-the-shoulder response whenever I asked why she didn't at least take the easy drive from our house 25 miles to the shore.

When I became a mother, I vowed that I would endeavor to fulfill all reasonable whims. And, thanks to Ludwig Bemelmans' Parisian-themed *Madeline* books, it didn't take long to find one. My daughter Chloé, who read each book until the pages creased, asked me if I'd show her the Eiffel Tower one day. When she turned six, I took her to Paris, and as we rounded a corner and crossed the Pont d'Alma, the celebrated landmark came into view. It was night and the lights sparkled like the Fourth of July. Chloé gasped. I watched the curiosity and wonder twirl in her eyes as she reconciled the cartoonish sketches from her bedtime stories with the shimmering, larger-than-life monument before her.

"It's so big!" she said.

Though I wanted to clutch her close to me forever, I hoped I'd also planted a seed of wanderlust in her, and that somehow I'd made her world a little bigger, too. But mostly, as a mother, I wanted Chloé to see that "someday" could become today.

*****

The woman in the elevator drops the phone back into her open purse, then interlaces her fingers, caressing the length of each before putting them back on her crutches. "I'm having *so* much trouble with my hands today," she says.

It's the second time she's said it, and the statement now feels more like an invitation to ask. I stare at my feet; the carpet; the rubber tips of her crutches. Saying nothing doesn't feel right, but is it OK to ask her what's wrong with her hands, or is it wrong to use the word *wrong*?

"So, what's going on there?" I ask, adding a quick jerk of my chin.

"I've been diagnosed with ALS," she says.

I'd expected her to say arthritis or another familiar name, but not a medically formidable acronym. I've heard of ALS but don't know enough to respond, so I just shake my head.

"Lou Gehrig's disease?" she prompts.

"I'm sorry," I say. "I don't know what that is."

She explains that ALS is the abbreviation for amyotrophic lateral sclerosis, a neuromuscular disease that attacks and degrades muscles and motor skills, like those in her hands and legs, until they atrophy and die.

The word die lingers in the air next to the hum of the elevator motor. A lump clogs my throat.

"How long ago were you diagnosed?" I finally ask.

"Nine months," she says.

"And you've had a second opinion?" I murmur.

She gives a half-laugh. "A second. A third. A fourth."

Another weighty silence hangs between us.

"Is this your first time in Paris?" I finally ask.

She nods.

"I've always dreamed of coming here," she says. "And I wanted to see it before I couldn't."

For the first time in the moment we've been together, I really look at her, and not her crutches. Under the halo of a small overhead light, and with the golden elevator trimming the backdrop, she looks posed like a portrait in a gilded frame. She's about 10 years older than I, 50ish. Her black hair parts in the middle and ripples against cheekbones that chisel sharp edges below her brown eyes and shade the hollows of her cheeks. Her skin gathers like a cinched sack at the outline of her rose-tinted lips, which hint at both a smile and something else I can't quite decipher. Stretching out my right hand instinctively, I introduce myself. She squeezes it harder than I expect and says her name is Leigh.

When we finally reach the fifth floor, the gate bangs open and I hold it while she shuffles toward her white-haired mother who beckons her daughter into outstretched arms. I step out, too, and the elevator gate slams behind us.

We say goodbye and I watch as Leigh's mother places one hand on the small of her daughter's back and the other over the rigid cuff clamped to her daughter's arm.

"I can do it, Mom," Leigh says, pushing ahead.

But her mom doesn't waver and pulls her daughter a little closer. Leigh lets her.

Watching them, I understand the only way they can conceivably bear their collective fear and grief is by doing it together. This mother's strength is like a punch to my gut. It's something I both admire and doubt I'd ever be able to summon.

Before she enters her room, Leigh turns back toward me.

"What's your favorite place in Paris?"

I'd just spent that morning wandering the familiar cobblestone streets that had awakened me years ago. Paris is my favorite place in Paris, I'd like to say.

Instead, I suggest Notre Dame Cathedral.

"There's a bronze star in front, set in the cobblestones," I tell her. "It's from there that all road distances in France are measured. The star is point zero, the starting point."

It was a place I had stood when I came to Paris as a young woman and dreamed about my road ahead. And it was there that I took Chloé during her first trip to Paris too, presenting her with the same idea: wishing her a future full of stars to wish upon and chase.

Leigh thanks me and closes her door, and I climb the final steps up to my room. Outside my window I see the peaks of ancient rooftops pierced by attic rooms, where lights flick on and off and occupants ebb and flow in life's familiar tableau.

And I see the crown of Notre Dame in the distance, below which I picture a mother placing her daughter's feet on a star, fulfilling a child's wish at the starting point of a very different kind of road.

Kimberley Lovato is a freelance writer whose work has appeared in print and online media, including National Geographic, AFAR, American Way, Delta Sky, Virginia Living, Marin Magazine, travelandleisure.com, bbc.com, frommers.com and lonelyplanet.com. Her essays have won awards and been anthologized in Best Women's Travel Writing for three straight years, while her book, Walnut Wine & Truffle Groves, received the Gold 2012 Lowell Thomas Award from the Society of American Travel Writers Foundation. www.kimberleylovato.com

THE PERFECT GIFT
Guatemala

After being crammed elbow-to-elbow on a ramshackle bus, I'm finally standing on the cobbled main road of Nebaj (pronounced Neh-bah). The tranquility of this small hamlet, nestled deep in the Cuchuamatanes Mountains of northern Guatemala, is a welcome relief after the hellish five-hour bus ride from Huehuetenango.

Streaks of rain bounce off the red, tiled roofs of weathered adobe buildings. A quiet plaza at the end of the street fronts a modest colonial church, while mist-shrouded emerald peaks are barely perceptible beyond the town. The cool air is heavy with the scent of damp pine needles.

Nebaj is the largest of three towns that encompass Guatemala's Ixil Triangle, one of the country's tiniest ethnic regions and the only place in the world where the Ixil language is spoken. Although it boasts access to stunning, semi-tropical landscapes and ancient Mayan culture, few tourists venture into this isolated region. But past journeys have taught me that off-the-beaten track destinations are often the most rewarding, so here I am.

As I walk into the plaza, I see dusky-skinned Mayan women crouched under canopies selling vegetables spread across linen cloths. They wear hand-woven blouses ornamented with intricate geometric patterns and dazzling, crimson skirts, while their raven hair is wrapped in braided strips of cloth and embellished with red and green pompoms.

This secluded borough is indescribably idyllic, but I've read that it bore witness to some of Guatemala's most brutal atrocities during the civil war of the 1980s. Human rights groups estimate that nearly a third of the region's 85,000 Ixil residents were either killed or displaced by the army in their campaign against local rebel guerillas.

Other than the chattering women trying to sell their produce and a couple of scrawny dogs, there is little sign of activity today. A barefoot Ixil woman wearing a scarlet *rebozo* (shawl) emerges through the rain and approaches me.

"You want to buy weavings, Señor?" she asks. "I sell from my home, very close to here." She is stout, with dark captivating eyes that match her long, braided hair.

"Maybe later," I tell her. "But first I need to find a hotel."

She recommends the Hotel Ixil at the end of the main road. We agree to meet in front of the hotel in an hour when she'll escort me to her house. I'm genuinely interested in looking at her weavings, but I'm even more curious to check out the home of a real Mayan. Before she leaves she says with a bashful smile that her name is Magdalena.

Exactly one hour later Magdalena is waiting outside the hotel entrance as promised. She leads me silently down a narrow gravel laneway to a modest one-room adobe hut with dirt floors. A young boy seated at a rickety table and chairs studies earnestly under a dim light bulb. The only other pieces of furniture are two narrow beds pushed against a wall. Squabbling chickens and a boisterous turkey scuttle around a rear courtyard. A wrinkled Mayan woman hunched in the corner prepares an enormous vat of peppery-scented *sopa* over an open fire. Beside her a young girl weaves a scarlet-colored blanket on a backstrap loom.

Taped to the wall inside her home is a faded photo of a young man in military fatigues. "Your husband?" I inquire.

"No, my brother. The army took him during war. My *esposo* left many months ago." She bites her lip and shrugs. "Many women like me in Nebaj. We make money only selling vegetables at market and selling weavings to the few *turistas* who come here. It is difficult, but… life goes on." She says this without a trace of self-pity.

Magdalena then pulls two large bags from underneath one of the beds and produces dozens of handmade weavings. One by one across the saggy beds she lays table runners, cotton tunics called *huipiles*, and wall hangings in a myriad of colors and patterns, across the saggy beds. Some of the designs are similar to the blouse she is wearing, while others are markedly different. Many have embroidered figures of birds and animals.

"You made these?" I ask.

"No," she replies. "I make some, but most made by other women. Some live in countryside so they give to me because I live in town." She shows me a piece of paper pinned to the back of each one with the name of its creator scrawled by hand.

I buy four table runners that are adorned with burgundy, jade and tan-colored bird figures, and a striking blue and green bag. I give Magdalena about $20, less than half what I would pay in the touristy markets at Chichicastenango and Panajachel. Still, $20 is a considerable amount here in the poorest region of this impoverished country.

She squeezes the bills tightly in her hand, as if she's afraid they will vanish. She holds her breath and watches intently when I pick up an additional weaving, a magenta wall hanging. I would love to add this brilliant piece to my collection, but my cash is running low so I decide against it.

I trudge back to my hotel with my newly acquired possessions. A fresh-faced young English couple is sitting in the courtyard who have recently arrived on a later bus from Santa Cruz del Quiche. They tell me their names are Alan and Claire, and. after a month of studying Español at a school in the vibrant colonial town of Antigua, they decided to explore Guatemala. Like me, they were intrigued to visit Nebaj after reading a favorable review in their guidebook.

"The outfits the locals wear look absolutely fabulous," Claire enthuses. "Do you know if there's any place around here we could buy some?"

"I know just such a place," I assure them. "In fact, if you like, I could take you there right now."

Magdalena looks startled when I knock on her door a few minutes later accompanied by Claire and Alan. "These are *turistas* from England," I tell her. "They are interested in buying weavings."

She recovers from her surprise and invites us inside, but not before she quickly re-attaches the elaborate head adornments that all Ixil women wear in public and when they receive visitors. I'm amazed that she is able to wrap the multiple ribbons of cloth and distinctive *pom-poms* around her flowing tresses in a matter of seconds.

Inside her home Magdalena shows the various weavings to her English guests, who are gob-smacked by the superior quality of the handcrafted articles laid out before them, not to mention the cheap prices. They acquire a dozen multicolored table runners, several vibrant wall hangings, and two floral embroidered *huipiles*. When they hand Magdalena $50 for their purchases, she looks overwhelmed. Her take today has probably been more than she makes in an average month.

As Claire and Alan are loading their goods into their packs Magdalena steps forward and squeezes my arm. The look of gratitude in her eyes is heart-rending.

After a quick siesta back at my hotel I head out in search of some dinner. The rain has just stopped; the wet cobblestone streets shimmer in the late afternoon sun. The Mayan women in the plaza are bundling up their unsold goods. Many have already started along dirt paths that lead up into the surrounding hillside back to their homes. A few macho young *hombres* re-enact the World Cup final on a dilapidated foosball table, while some giggling *chicas* look on from the church steps.

Down a narrow lane I discover the Maya Inca restaurant. Candle-lit tables and oil paintings of local mountain vistas lend the place some pastoral charm and, unlike the grubby *comedor* I checked out across from my hotel, it has a real wood floor.

The owner is Peruvian-born Alberto Heredia, an affable English-speaking *caballero*. He tells me that he moved to Nebaj several years ago, married an Ixil woman, and together they opened this restaurant. On his recommendation, I order *pollo con pera crema*, chicken with pear sauce, a Peruvian specialty.

After the *delicioso* main course, Alberto brings me robust Guatemalan coffee and syrupy pastries. Since the only two other customers have left, he accepts my invitation and joins me for dessert.

"I enjoy to meet people from outside," he explains. "For years we receive no foreigners, because of the problems. Maybe you know? Now a few come, but we need more, for the economy."

I hesitate to press him for details about the civil war, but I can't resist the chance to get firsthand information from someone who lived through those tragic events. "Is it true that government troops killed a lot of people here?"

He takes a deep breath. "*Si*. There were rebels here, but the army also killed innocent civilians. Many men were forced to join the army and fight their own people." I think of Magdalena's brother. "They destroyed two dozen villages." He pauses to collect himself. "In one town they put all the men in a church and shot them. Thousands were killed. Many fled north to Mexico."

"Didn't the government and the rebels recently sign a treaty?" I ask.

"Several years ago," Alberto tells me. "But many locals still haven't returned. Some villages are still not fully rebuilt." He lowers his cup before continuing. "These are proud people. They want only to practice their way of life and live in peace, but for 500 years they are treated badly. They are... I can't remember the English word... *traumatismo*."

"Traumatized," I answer.

"It is very sad, *señor*."

As I stroll through the hushed village back to my hotel I pass a few locals, each of whom acknowledges me with a sincere *buenas noches*. For the first time I understand the sadness in their eyes. I hope that one day this place will transform into the Shangri-La that its people deserve.

The next morning, I wake early to the sound of chirping birds. *El sol* has emerged to bathe the nearby forest and the town, which is now full of life. My bus doesn't leave until the afternoon, so I resolve to take advantage of the spring-like weather and explore the countryside.

I meander along a dirt road and cross a bridge that leads to a footpath along a stream lined with tin-roofed houses and tiny verdant gardens. A sweaty farmer tending corn crops next to a rustic bungalow grins and waves his straw hat. A burro is tied to a fence in front. As I saunter further into the woodlands the flora becomes increasingly thicker; palm trees, giant pines and alders wrapped in lush orchids surround me. Laughing children pop out from behind giant hedges, only to disappear if I venture too close.

After awhile I stop beside a miniature waterfall, and reflect on my stay in Nebaj. In only two days I've acquired an immense admiration for the people here. How the Ixil have remained so modest and welcoming after all they've experienced — indeed how they've survived at all — is astonishing. As I nod off next to the calming rush of water, I realize that my earlier hunch was correct. Since arriving in Guatemala two weeks ago, I've wandered through gorgeous colonial cities, haggled at raucous outdoor markets, and witnessed daunting volcanoes, but it's this humble *puebla* that will leave the strongest impression.

I wake with a start an hour later, realizing that my bus will leave soon.

Back at my hotel, I'm frantically stuffing clothes into my pack when I hear someone knock at my door.

Magdalena stands in the doorway with her arms folded, her gaze fixed on the ground. She wears the same outfit as yesterday, except for a brilliant weaving draped across her shoulder.

I'm taken aback by her presence. "*Hola*," I finally manage.

"*Hola*," she replies. Blushing, she takes the weaving off her shoulder and places it in my hand. She bows and is gone.

I stare down at the weaving. It's the same one I had wanted to buy yesterday. A single word is scribbled on a label: Magdalena.

Rick's passion for travel was ignited 25 years ago when he signed up for an international student exchange program in Turkey, an eye-opening experience that revealed the outside world is a fascinating place worth exploring. Since then, his wanderlust has taken him to Europe, Mexico, Central America, Vietnam, Ecuador, China, where he spent a memorable year teaching English, and most recently to Morocco. Rick resides in Vancouver, Canada, where he writes for various travel publications.

JANNA GRABER

MY FRIEND, THE ENEMY
Berlin, Germany

Standing at the edge of Alexanderplatz, I watch Berlin pass by. A young man with dreadlocks whirls his bike around an elderly couple walking arm in arm, while across the street, a man selling balloons counts out change in the warm summer air.

It's 3 p.m., and we have been on a quest. My friend TJ has promised us curry wurst. Not just any curry wurst, but some of the city's best. The sausages served with spicy tomato sauce are a favorite here in Berlin, so my boyfriend, Ben, and I have followed our friend's eager pace to the heart of the city.

But the sight of the crowd-filled square, filled with white tent vendors and brightly-covered advertising, stops me in my tracks. Can this really be the Alexanderplatz that I remember? I see the iconic TV tower that looms over the square and the same circular time clock, but everything else looks different.

Up ahead, I glimpse Ben and TJ round a corner. Not wanting to lose them, I jog to catch up. TJ's tall frame helps keep him in my sight. He is the perfect picture of a successful Prussian businessman: tall, middle-aged good looks, perfectly polished ways. Yet, no matter how many times I have seen him like this, it still gives me a start.

Berlin has changed a great deal in the past 25 years. For that matter, so has TJ. There was a time when this man was considered my "enemy."

*****

The Cold War was in its last dying breaths when I met TJ in the winter of 1987. I had been studying in Vienna, and decided to do some traveling during winter break. While most of my friends traveled south to Italy or Greece, I signed up for a two-week "exchange" trip to a university in East Berlin. We would attend lectures and experience life in East Germany.

During one boring lecture on "surplus value" from the communist viewpoint, I began to doodle in my notebook. A young East German student who was sitting nearby leaned over and asked what I was drawing.

It was an exchange that would affect us both.

The young man had a German name that I was unfamiliar with, so he just laughed and said, "Call me TJ." He was a rising star being pushed to the forefront at the university. Like many of the students there, he was a member of the FDJ, the communist youth party. He believed in the ideals of communism and was working for a better East Germany.

I, on the other hand, was a 20-year-old kid from the American West who barely knew what communism was. We obviously had our differences.

While many of the other East German students looked at me with distrust, TJ viewed me with curiosity. Because we couldn't talk openly, where disapproving Communist Party members would see, TJ asked if we could meet outside one night. In the freezing cold of a German winter, we began to talk.

At first, we debated politics and economics, often disagreeing. But as our nightly meetings continued, the conversation gave way to the normal topics of youth: music, the future and life. And in those topics, we saw eye to eye.

We were like any other good college friends — except that we were not supposed to be friends. The party leaders kept their eyes on us, making sure we didn't get too close.

*****

Alexanderplatz doesn't look anything like the town square that I remember from those communist days. Today, there are throngs of tourists and locals rushing to work. Parents push strollers, while laughing children run up ahead.

I soak it all in while eating my curry wurst, trying to reconcile the changes.

When I first walked this cobblestone 27 years ago, it had been gray and drab. The square had been clean and quiet then, filled with Russian and East German soldiers in pressed uniforms, their fresh faces full of youth. I had watched schoolchildren hurrying quietly across the square for school, and young men wearing Russian fur hats jaunting off to their state-guaranteed places of employment.

My pockets were full of Ost-Marks back then, but there was nothing to buy. Now, neon signs and huge billboards splash with color and promises of a good life, if I'd only buy this or that.

Today Alexanderplatz looks like most big city squares. There are the taggings of bored young men, dropped fast-food wrappers and abandoned newspapers. Free men, it seems, can say and do whatever they want. Yet in truth, free men can be messy.

Filled with curry wurst, we leave the crowds behind and hop into TJ's Mercedes. We drive past the Brandenburg Gate, and I can't stop the lump that fills my throat.

"Sometimes, I go out of my way just to drive by the Brandenburg Gate," TJ admits. "It makes me feel good just to know that I can walk through it whenever I want."

I understand completely.

The famous Gate once sat in the middle of a forbidden no-man's land, like an abandoned island between two warring worlds. I had stood at the fence looking at the Gate from the east side, which was patrolled by East German soldiers, and hated that border for the pain it caused. Now the Brandenburg Gate is once again a thing of beauty.

The traffic is bumper to bumper as we drive on to Checkpoint Charlie, now a tourist attraction. Back then, I wasn't allowed to cross into West Berlin. It was part of my visa agreement with the East German school. But I had seen Checkpoint Charlie from the eastern side, a lonely gate between two very different worlds. I belonged in one world; TJ belonged to the other.

Today, we are at the Checkpoint Charlie Museum. It is a hot July day, and the museum's tiny rooms are packed with tourists. I follow TJ and Ben as they move through the exhibits.

In one room, I read about the Wall, when and how it went up, and how it changed life in Berlin. Then we move on to exhibits about those who tried to escape the east using secret car compartments, underground tunnels, and even an air balloon. My breathing gets faster as I realize this is not just an exhibit, but a time that TJ and even I lived through. How strange to see your personal history on the walls of a museum.

Suddenly, I am very annoyed. "It's too hot in here!" I complain to TJ. And indeed the room temperature must be in the 80s. I am sweating in my summer dress.

"If the Germans can figure out how to make great cars, why can't they figure out how to cool a room?" I mumble angrily.

Then I realize. It is much more that is making me angry. How I hated that damn Wall.

*****

From Checkpoint Charlie, we move on to see more of the city. The streets of Berlin seem brighter than I remember. Perhaps it is the glare of the tall, mirrored buildings that surround me, their grand entrances gathering in and then spewing out streams of harried businessmen. It could be the metallic sheen of all the Mercedes and BMWs that fill the roads, their shiny wealth a reminder of how this city has reinvented itself as the vibrant capital of a reunited Germany.

As the traffic inches forward, we pass another building, the Stars and Stripes waving out front.

"You remember when…?" I ask.

"Yup," TJ smirks.

During my last weeks as a student in communist East Germany, several other American students and I were invited to a "Mexican dinner" at the U.S. Embassy. I hadn't had Mexican food for more than a year, and my mouth had watered at the sound of it. The thought of being around other Americans also offered a strange relief, so I immediately agreed to go.

Eagerly, the other students and I made our way down the embassy buffet line, piling food onto our plates and opening can after can of tasty American soda.

"What have they been teaching you at the university?" an American Embassy official casually asked. "Not much," we answered. "Just stuff about the communist economic system."

"Who did you speak to?" another asked. "What have you seen?"

With sinking dread, I realized that we were being "questioned." This time, it was my own paranoid government that was fishing for information. I didn't say a thing.

Instead, I slipped out and into the other room where the buffet line was still spread out. I grabbed several cans of soda for TJ and stuffed them into my coat. Later that night, I pulled them out of my pocket for TJ, who laughed as he fumbled to open the unfamiliar can lids. He liked several of the drinks, but thought root beer was terrible.

"Look, this is where the Wall once stood," TJ exclaims, drawing my attention back to the present. He points out a narrow, brick-lined path along the road. It is a small, yet vibrant reminder of the not-so-distant past. The Wall was so frightening then; now it is simply part of the street.

*****

Time never stands still, and eventually my studies in East Berlin ended. The day came when I had to leave the gray-filled city behind. In a misting rain that mirrored my mood, I lugged my suitcase out to the waiting bus, wondering how you say goodbye to someone forever.

TJ hugged me and then slipped a little piece of paper with the address of his grandmother into my hand, while I tried to hide the tears that kept flooding into my eyes. "You can't write to me, but you can write to my grand-mother. I don't think they will check her mail. Be careful what you write," he said. "But we will keep in touch."

I tried to read the emotions on my friend's face as the bus pulled out, but saw only stone. Later, he told me how difficult that goodbye had been, knowing that I was headed to a place he could never visit.

But that was then; this is now. TJ is now the CEO of a huge international company. Life has opened new doors, and my friend has gone through them with gusto.

It's just one more change in a thousand.

****

Those changes began back in 1989. East Germany was growing weary of repression and restless for reform. Thousands of people began to meet at local churches, marching for change and holding peaceful prayer ser-vices. A force began to grow that could not be stopped.

During this time, TJ's letters stopped filling my mail-box. Like thousands around him, he was growing impatient for change. The system wasn't working; something had to be altered. But my friend couldn't write the truth: that he had climbed over the German Embassy fence in Prague to defect, but then reconsidered, thinking of all he would leave behind. In the end, he had climbed back over the fence and went home to work for transformation in East Germany.

So did thousands of others. The protests kept coming, the pressure built up and East German leaders began to weaken.

Then in November, the miracle happened. I sat on the living room floor in Denver as live images were broadcast from East Berlin. Thousands of East Germans poured through the open Wall and into West Berlin. Young men danced on the concrete barrier that had once been forbidden; a flower was presented to a border guard. Hope, excitement and thankfulness filled the faces that had once seemed so distant.

A few weeks later, I got a small package in the mail. It was a piece of the Wall that I had once hated. And I knew exactly who it was from.

Two months later, TJ was standing in the kitchen of my American home. I was cutting lettuce to make tacos when I stopped and stared at my friend: Sometimes the world changes faster than our ability to comprehend it.

As the years went by, TJ remained a close friend. One of my closest, in fact. He celebrated from afar when I got married, and then swung me around in person on the day I told him I was pregnant with my first child.

He carried that child on his shoulders while I waddled around pregnant with my second when he visited us another summer. When my third child was little, TJ helped him carve pumpkins on a visit during Halloween.

I, too, have visited Germany as often as I could. On this trip, we have come to meet the love of his life – the woman who will soon become his wife.

The years have passed quickly for both of us, as my children grew and TJ moved up through the corporate world.

When my personal world fell apart, it was TJ who called to make sure I was all right during the awful divorce. His soothing voice came often via phone from across the ocean. "You're going to be OK," he reassured me one night when I could not even pull myself from my bed.

I think of those times now as we drive through Berlin. "You were my lifeline," I say to TJ, interrupting his conversation with Ben.

"What's a lifeline?" he asks.

"Someone who saves a person from drowning," I reply. TJ nods and understands.

*****

We have two more stops in our whirlwind Berlin adventure. The first is to visit TJ's parents. I have gotten to know them over the years, and I'm eager to see them again.

They live in a beautiful new home in the suburbs of East Berlin, and they've invited us for coffee. TJ's mom serves us a strawberry pie in her flower-filled garden. I dust off my German and we laugh and reminisce. I ask her to tell me about "those times."

She said she and her husband where just 21 and 26 in 1961 when the Wall went up. Both teachers, they had been at a summer camp when someone came and told them a Wall had gone up. No one could believe it. They worried about their parents and hurried back home to make sure they were OK. It had been only 16 years since the end of WWII and their parents were afraid that war was starting again.

"Life certainly changed when the Wall went up," says TJ's mom. "But not all was bad in the DDR (East Germany). We lived, we went to school, and we had families."

She talks then of when the Wall came down. How everyone was rejoicing and happy, drinking *Sekt* and dancing. The Champagne bottles littered the ground. She and TJ's dad went out, but the crowds were so crazy that they went right back home.

But all wasn't rosy. Her brother lost his job soon after. She had taught elementary school for more than 25 years, but still had to retest to become a teacher again. Still, things eventually got better.

Better indeed. I look around at the beautiful home and their smiling faces. Yes, life is good now in eastern Berlin.

*****

I want to see a good view of Berlin — all of it — so TJ heads the car to the Reichstag. Home to Germany's Parliament, it is a beautiful, stately building that immediately commands respect.

TJ treats us to dinner at Käfer, the award-winning restaurant at the top of the Reichstag. As we savor German beer and cuisine, we watch it grow dark across the city. "This is the western part of the city," TJ says, pointing one way, "and that is the east."

I struggle to see the differences, to locate something familiar, but I can't. At night, from atop this symbol of a united Germany, it looks like one big beautiful city — which is what it is.

We are some of the last people in the restaurant, and the Reichstag's magnificent dome area is almost empty. The guards are getting ready to shut down for the night, but TJ convinces them to let us go up the circular ramp that leads to the top.

At the top, we lay back on the seats in the center and look up at the night sky through the glass dome. Everything is silent, and it is surreal to be here in this beautiful land where so much has happened.

We joke as we wind our way down the ramps again. There's an exhibit on Berlin at the bottom. TJ finds a photo of a Michael Jackson concert in West Berlin. The concert promoters had set up the speakers so the walled-off eastern side of the city could hear. TJ and his dad had gone to a car dealership near the border so TJ could listen to the concert.

I laugh when I realize that I never got to attend a Michael Jackson concert, but the kid from East Berlin did.

*****

As we pack to head home to America, we make plans to meet again with TJ soon. At the airport, he hugs us goodbye and then rushes off to work. I smile and follow Ben toward our gate, wondering if TJ knows how proud of him I am.

As the plane rises over Berlin, I press my face against the window, watching the buildings and people grow tiny. It's so green below, lush with trees and gardens — a beautiful city on any account.

Then sitting back in my seat, I notice the man beside me open up his newspaper. There, on the front cover, is a scene that I have viewed all too often in the last years. Young Arab men stare at the camera, their eyes full of hate, their voices raised against America.

Once again, I have an enemy.

A familiar worried ache fills my stomach, and I wonder about the young men in the picture. Do they like deep blue skies, or the laughter of small children? Do they know that I do?

Will we ever see eye to eye?

Then I think of Berlin and TJ. It is a present reality that I never would have dreamed. Yes indeed, people can change. Even countries can change.

Berlin gives me hope for the future.

Janna Graber is an American travel journalist, editor and producer who has covered travel in more than 38 countries. She fell in love with exploring other countries and cultures while studying abroad in Austria, and has been hooked ever since. She is the managing editor at GoWorldTravel.com, and has written for Parade, Reader's Digest, Outside, Chicago Tribune and many more. Read more of her work at jannagraber.com or follow her on Twitter @AColoradoGirl.

THE SHORTCUT
Japan

"You must go to Temple 24," said the naked stranger at the Kuroshio Baths on the island of Shikoku. "It can't be skipped."

We were the only two customers in the women's section of the hot springs. For nearly an hour, we had been soaking and chatting, neck-deep in a steaming pool overlooking the Pacific Ocean.

"Sorry?" I said, "I'm not sure what you mean."

My Japanese was functional, but nuance was a long way off. Was she giving me travel advice, spiritual advice or something more? Why was she suggesting that I add to my already-strenuous walking schedule?

"You absolutely must go to Cape Muroto to Temple 24," she repeated.

"*Doshite*? Why?" I asked, as politely as I could.

"Because Cape Muruto is a very special place," she said, with conviction.

"Have you walked all the way down there yourself?" I asked.

"Walked? Oh my goodness, no. I'm not a walker. But I've visited Hotsumisakiji many times by car."

She was a Japanese woman in her early-50s. I gathered that she was married, lived nearby, had time on her hands, and came to the hot springs regularly for an afternoon of relaxation, the way some people might go to the cinema or play golf.

I was an American woman in my late-60s trekking around the island of Shikoku, following the 1,200-kilometer (745-mile) pilgrimage trail known as the 88 Temples. I had a husband, family and friends back in Connecticut.

Unlike the stranger, I had stopped at the Kuroshio Baths as a once-in-a-lifetime experience. I had been reading billboards for several days touting the virtues of these hot springs. As a tired and sweaty hiker, I couldn't resist. But the Kuroshio Baths were a detour. I would soon be back on the pilgrimage trail, ankle deep in dust or mud.

"You will not regret it," said the stranger, stepping out of the bath and reaching for a towel.

Her wet black hair was piled on top of her head.

My guidebook had made it clear that walking all the way to the tip of Cape Muruto was problematic. The trail was isolated, with almost no accommodations for 40 miles or more.

"You cannot have come all this way and not see Cape Muruto," continued the woman, drying herself off.

She had known from the get-go that I was a pilgrim, an *O-Henro*. No doubt she had seen my identifying uniform, the traditional white vest and conical straw hat, hanging in the outer room of the bath.

"That is very unusual. A foreign lady, alone, doing the 88 Temples on foot," she had said. "Quite unusual."

She didn't add "at your age," but perhaps she was thinking it.

I had explained to her in my halting Japanese that I would be spending the night at Yakuoji, Temple 23, not far from the Kuroshio Baths. I had already called and made a reservation with the temple monks.

"A reservation? That's not hard to change," said the stranger, now partly dressed and running a hairdryer over her straight hair.

"They are expecting me for the evening meal as well as lodging," I said.

"My husband knows those monks at Yakuoji very well. He will explain that you are not coming."

"*Sumimasen, ga*, excuse me, but...." I said.

I tried to explain my decision once again. I had already soaked away most of the afternoon in the baths. At best I would arrive at Temple 23 before dinner if I didn't dilly-dally. Then the next day, instead of heading straight south to the Cape, I was planning to take a bus west into northern Kochi prefecture and start walking again at Temple 28. I would leave Cape Muruto and its sister temples, numbers 24 to 27, to more hardy souls.

I wasn't sure the woman heard my explanation over the *whish-whish* of the hairdryer. But when she turned it off, she smiled at me and said, "So it is settled, right?"

I tried to parse the sentence. Settled? What was settled?

I finished getting dressed, putting on fresh underwear, a clean T-shirt and my dirty hiking pants. I only had two pairs with me, both dirty. I finished off with the white vest and conical hat.

"Are you Buddhist?" she asked.

I didn't have the vocabulary to clarify that I was a Unitarian.

"No, I just respect Buddhist culture," I answered.

"Then you will never regret going to Hotsumisakiji."

I knew that Temple 24 had historical significance. Kobo Daishi, the founder of Shingon Buddhism, had achieved enlightenment in a cave somewhere in the vicinity of Hotsumisakiji sometime in the 9th century. In fact, the prophet's common nickname, *Kukai*, probably refers to the meeting of the sky and the sea that he experienced at Cape Muruto. Temple 24 certainly sounded like a cool place.

Too bad I was going to miss it.

I was still confused as to why my bath companion assumed that she had gotten me to change my mind.

I ran a comb quickly through my hair, but the humidity of the hot springs had left me with wild curls. I put the comb back in a recycled plastic Lawson's bag, on top of my dirty T-shirt. I checked to make sure I had all my belongings. Living out of a backpack isn't complicated, but I had learned to always make sure I didn't leave behind any of the items I depended on: my cell phone, my poncho, a map, Band-Aids, safety pins and my journal.

The friendly stranger was still talking to me non-stop while she primped in front of the mirror, carefully applying a fresh coat of lipstick and dabs of moisturizer in strategic places. Finally she was ready, dressed in a simple, but elegant, beige silk pantsuit, with a coffee-colored scarf. We returned our towels to the matron at the main desk. Then I picked up my wooden walking stick, which I had left outside the door, and I was just about to say goodbye.

"Please wait here for my husband," the woman said. "He is finishing up in the men's bath."

In a few minutes, a Japanese man with a boy's face came out of the building. He looked benign and relaxed, like a dolphin who had spent the afternoon in a lazy lagoon.

"Yes, of course," he said, after his wife had taken him aside. He bowed, and in a mixture of English and Japanese explained their plan.

"We will be delighted to drive you to the Cape Muruto temple. This is a good thing."

"You mean, you will drive me to Temple 24 and then drive me back to Yakuoji where I have a reservation?"

"No, no. We will stop at Yakuoji and tell them you are going to the Cape Muruto temple with us, and the monks will be pleased for you."

I assumed that the couple were devout Buddhists who wanted to share their practices with me.

I had no compunction about hitching a ride with these kindly people, but I didn't want to get stuck at a distant destination with no shelter. Cape Muruto was known for fierce winds and sudden storms.

"That's very kind, but you see, I have no place to stay down there."

"Afterward we will drive you to our home. We have a guest room and many pilgrims have slept there. You would be most welcome. Please, come."

I could see an exciting detour being dangled in front of my eyes.

Both of them looked at me with gentle smiles. I had a good feeling about these people.

"Really? You would do this for me?" I asked. "*Doozo*" said the husband.

He gestured to a shiny white Mercedes parked in a shady corner of the parking lot.

Although the pores of my skin were probably the cleanest they had ever been, my hiking pants were covered with grass stains and traces of lunchtime *onigiri* purchased at a convenience store. I couldn't remember if these were also the pants upon which I had spilled a bottle of Qoo, a fruity beverage that I frequently found in Japanese vending machines. The soles of my Gore-Tex boots were corrugated with mud. I hesitated before getting in.

"*Notte kudasai*, please take a seat," said the husband, politely, relieving me of my backpack and stick.

The minute I stepped into the car, little flakes of mud fell onto the floor mats like shavings of chocolate on a vanilla ice cream cone. Neither the husband nor wife seemed to notice. Nor did they pay attention when I knocked my conical hat askew on the door. I caught a quick glimpse of myself in the rear view mirror. With my hair frizzy from the steamy bath, I looked vaguely buffoonish, a cross between a bag lady and Coco the Clown.

I reflected on the elegance of the wife's outfit, her clean fingernails and well-coiffed hair. I thought of her saying that her husband knew the temple monks very well. Perhaps the husband was a high-ranking Buddhist priest. I glanced at him as he was coming around to the right-side driver's seat. He was wearing an open-collared sports shirt, chino pants and soft leather shoes. He looked more like a tennis player than a man of the cloth.

"Are you a *bokushi*?" I asked, as soon he as was nestled on the white leather seat.

"Me? Oh, not at all. Me, a priest?"

His wife giggled. Then they started to laugh heartily. Obviously I had made some sort of joke.

"But you know the monks well?" I continued.

"I know everyone in Kochi prefecture," he said. "And almost everyone in Tokushima prefecture as well."

I could see a slice of his big grin in the mirror.

I tried to imagine what kind of person would know a lot of people. A politician? A drug-dealer? A *yakuza*? Did criminals know monks well enough to call them on the phone? The man looked more like a mischievous school boy than a person with connections to organized crime.

"We like to help the walking pilgrims," he explained. "To share Shikoku with them."

"Have you ever done the 88 Temple Pilgrimage?" I asked.

"Never on foot," he said. "I am too lazy. But I have visited every single temple many times by motorcycle. I love motorcycles."

It turned out that he owned several businesses all dealing with motorcycles and motorcycle parts. He also said he traveled occasionally to the United States.

"You go there to work?" I asked.

"Oh, no. I'm not that kind of businessman. No suit or tie. No briefcase. Never."

He looked at me in his rear view mirror and his eyes were smiling.

"I am casual guy," he said in English.

"I go to California to surf," he continued. "And Hawaii, too."

"But you can surf quite well here in Shikoku," I said, gesturing out the window at the Pacific.

"Yes, but like you, I need a change of scenery now and then, right?"

"Yes, of course."

"Travel is a way to exercise the body and feed the soul, no? That's perhaps why you are walking in Japan also?"

He continued talking for a while in rapid-fire Japanese, probably assuming my comprehension was better than it was. I understood about a third of what he said to me and almost nothing of what he said to his wife. I eventually concluded that together they were speaking a local dialect.

Mostly I just sat back and let the words flow over me as if my brain were a smooth rock in a stream, slightly mossy and cool.

The Mercedes air conditioner was working nicely.

The wife was already planning dinner.

"We'll stop at the fish market on the way back. You can eat ALL Japanese food?" she asked me in standard Japanese.

"Yes," I said enthusiastically. "But, well, the only thing is....I don't really like *natto* (fermented soy beans)."

"I am Japanese and I don't like *natto* either," said the husband with a guffaw from the driver's seat. "It smells like baby diapers."

It's moments like this that I travel for. Not for museums or spectacles or the Seven Wonders. But for conversations with strangers who have a sense of humor.

I tried to imagine what my family back home would think if they could have seen me whizzing across the Japanese countryside with two people whose names I didn't know, but whose spirit I would never forget.

Sometimes I looked out the car window. We passed appliance stores and baseball diamonds, nurseries and supermarkets. Then there were small wooded areas and patchwork farms, all bordered by volcanic hills and the blue Pacific Ocean. From time to time, the wife identified vistas or places, or the husband told stories of their drives around the island.

We were in the car for at least two hours. When I looked on the map, I was not sure why an 80-kilometer journey took so long. Later I realized that we must have eventually taken the Minamiawa Sun Line, a scenic highway that winds through spectacular countryside. Macaque monkeys played along the side of the road. Very few cars or trucks passed by in either direction.

When we reached the tip of the Cape, the husband parked the Mercedes and we walked up to Temple 24, the famous Hotsumisakiji.

Much to my surprise, neither the husband nor wife rang the temple bell or clapped their hands in *gassho*. They spent hardly any time reciting the sutras or lighting candles. When I started to dawdle near the gold statue of the reclining Buddha, the couple urged me to hurry along.

"The temple will soon close," they explained. "We can't linger."

I was puzzled that we had driven so far and yet spent so little time. Surely they would have known that the temple closed in the late afternoon.

"We've got to run to the *Nookyoosho* and get your temple book stamped," said the husband.

In the excitement of arriving, I had almost forgotten this pilgrimage ritual. At each of the 88 Temples, one pays a small fee and receives a stamp to indicate that he or she has visited the temple. We went back to the car and I retrieved my small pilgrim ledger from my backpack and waited at the Temple Stamping Office.

Meanwhile, the husband went off to find a vending machine. A few minutes later, he returned with some welcome bottles of spring water. I was still waiting in line. A bevy of chattering "bus" pilgrims had preceded me. Finally, after a wrinkled old monk stamped Temple 24's emblem into my book and signed the page with a beautiful calligraphic hand, we were ready to go.

"You must see the view. This is our favorite part," said the wife.

"Yes, it gives you the good feeling of being alive," said the husband. "Please enjoy it."

We bounded down to the overlook across the road. We stood on the precarious edge of the cliff at Cape Muruto and faced the thrashing Pacific. Sky and sea, *kukai*, indeed. The fierce blue heaven arched seamlessly into the equally fierce blue ocean.

It was pretty spectacular.

"We need to get to the fish market,'' said the wife, suddenly.

"Right," said the husband.

We scrambled back up to the temple just as the gates were closing. After the husband dropped a few coins in the collection box, we got back in the Mercedes and drove a half-hour to a town whose name I didn't catch.

The fish market was doing a brisk business.

"Not that one," the wife said to the fishmonger, as she chose fish after fish, six varieties in all. "That one over there."

An American-style supermarket was nearby. The husband maneuvered the shopping cart as if it were a motorcycle, happily turning corners at top speed, while the wife selected vegetables and fruits slowly and me-thodically.

We headed back out to the countryside, pulling up to a beautiful home, where they showed me the guest room. There was soon an immaculate white futon spread out on the floor.

As the wife prepared dinner, the husband talked to me about growing up on Shikoku.

"I grew up right here in Kochi. We didn't have much money," he said, fiddling with the remote control on his wide-screen TV. "And I wasn't a very good student. So I have been luckier than anyone ever imagined. I exceeded my parents' expectations. And my in-laws' expectations as well."

After a delicious dinner with much laughter and lively conversation, I got up my courage to ask why they offered perfect strangers such hospitality.

"Not perfect strangers. Pilgrims only," said the wife, as she cleared off the dozens of delicate little porcelain plates from which we had eaten.

"It is just what we do," said the husband. "We have so very much. We are fortunate to have this home and cars and leisure time. And we care a lot for Shikoku. It is our birthplace. Why not share these things?"

I pressed them for their address so I could send a thank-you letter and gifts from the States.

"No need," they said, "We are just happy to have met you."

"But...." I tried to plead further.

"Just consider this day and evening as *osettai*, the Shikoku tradition of charity."

They refused to give me any other information.

I decided later that the temple this couple really showed me was not physical or touristic or geographical. It was metaphorical.

We didn't need to spend a great deal of time at Temple 24. My hosts took me to a much more significant sacred space.

Devotees of the great religions have built impressive places all over the world. I've been fortunate to have visited many of them and taken photos and read their histories. *How Chartres was Built. The Mysteries of Stonehenge. The Story of Machu Pichu.*

But after that chance meeting at the Furoshio Baths, I learned once again that, for me, the most important sacred spaces are not in the guidebooks. They are the sacred spaces created when human beings reach out to other human beings and pull them into their lives, even for just a short time. Who hasn't felt enormously blessed when a stranger offers a meal, a smile, a conversation or a shared laugh? What traveler hasn't felt privileged, even awed, when a native extends an invitation to his home?

During the day and night I spent with this delightful and unusual couple, I felt as if I were sheltered in a sort of holy building, something with a dome or a nave or a minaret. A place built entirely on trust and good will. A place that existed only because of a sort of grace. Like a rainbow or a sunset.

The next day, we ate breakfast together in the kitchen and then the husband took off on his motorcycle. The wife proceeded to drive me to a nearest point where the pilgrim path intersected with the road so I could continue my long, quiet and sometimes lonely journey.

"Before noon, you'll be at Temple 25 and by mid-afternoon you'll be at Temple 26," she said, "*Ki otsu-kete*. Take care."

She waved and she was gone.

I stood by the side of the road and bowed gratefully into the warm Shikoku wind.

Gabriella Brand's short stories, essays and poetry have appeared in Room Magazine, StepAway, Mom Egg, Chordite, The Christian Science Monitor, and Three Element Review. One of her stories was nominated for a Pushcart Prize in 2013. She divides her time between New England, where she teaches three foreign languages, and Quebec, where she writes, canoes and daydreams. She prefers to travel by foot, all over the world.

THE GUIDE WITH THE GOLDEN TEETH
Albania

It is early morning in the ship's Vista Lounge. Passengers cluster. Curtains sway with the sea. I am awake, but thanks to the softness of the lounge's velour chair, I keep remembering sleep.

"You on the Kickin' Corfu tour?" says a man with a backpack and an aluminum-and-rubber cane. Um, no, I say. Shore excursion No. 6. I'm going to Albania.

"Albania?" he repeats. It's a country that always seems to come with a question.

That's right, I say. Albania.

"Well, better git with your group," he says, giving me a suspicious stare.

I don't tell him more, but in fact I've always been curious about this tiny Eastern European nation. Maybe it's from reading the comic strip Dilbert, with its made-up outpost, "Elbonia." Elbonia mirrors Albania in seeming wildly out-of-the-loop.

Albania lived under the thumb of a communist dictator named Enver Hoxha from the end of World War II until his death in 1985 (and the fall of communism here in 1991). Ruled before that by Romans, Byzantines and Ottomans, the nation under Hoxha got detached from the world. A map I looked at from the 1950s showed it as a blank area, not a country.

But color is coming back to the now-independent free-market democracy. A bit of the Balkan Peninsula, it's only slightly larger than Maryland. But there's variety inside that space, including a mountain-studded interior and an unspoiled Adriatic coastline. Travelers, like me, who long for places that don't yet have a Starbucks are starting to take notice.

It is my chance, I think, to fill in the blank.

*****

As soon as I leave my velour chair on the ship things start happening fast. I'm required to retrieve my passport from the purser's office. We're the only shore excursion tour group that's changing countries. And I'm tagged with an orange sticker that says "Holland America Line Oosterdam No. 6."

Is this in case I'm lost? I feel like Paddington the Bear.

Holland America Line's' MS Oosterdam is in the port of Kerkira, Corfu, for a single day. Most passengers are walking around town or are on 3- or 4-hour local excursions like "Panoramic Corfu" ($54) or "Corfu and Mon Repo Palace" ($59).

My "Albanian Adventure" tour is listed as lasting a total of seven hours. And it's pricey. I can barely afford the $221 fee. "Strenuous," warns the cruise line brochure. "Roads are bumpy. Insect repellent is strongly recommended."

All of this makes me think that two, maybe three other passengers will leave the clean and comfortable cocoon of the ship and sign up. But as we roar out of the port, my orange No. 6 bus is completely full.

Up front is our Albanian tour guide, a tanned middle-aged man with golden edges around his upper row of teeth. When he tells us his name, we nod. But it's a difficult sound. Later I sneak a look at his badge: Vangjel Xhani of SIPA Tours. Xhani lives in the capital city, Tirana. He has two backup careers. "I am also a professor and a doctor," he tells us.

The bus is already stopping. "OK," says Xhani, "now we get on board our ship. Albania next stop."

"Look dad," says a girl of about 10. "We're going inside that blimp." The ship —actually a hovercraft — has a gently rounded shape that makes it seem like it's been inflated. Instead of carrying us across the Ionian Sea, it looks liable to float straight up. Ionian Lines' Flying Dolphin, says the hand-painted sign.

Everyone seems nervous settling in on the Flying Dolphin in part because the upholstered seat-backs flop forward if you touch them. We tourists are crammed in next to local commuters who have brought knapsacks full of groceries aboard. When the Dolphin starts its engines, it makes a noise that's similar to a blender with the "pulse" button pushed down.

As we hum and bounce our way across the water, two government officials wearing caps and T-shirts work their way through a rainbow stack of passports, stamping each and calling out the name of its owner. You're supposed to get up from your floppy seat to collect it. For lazy passengers who only shout their name, passports are tossed.

Soon we are seeing Albania for the first time through a churning mist created by the Flying Dolphin. It is not simple to describe.

The resort town of Saranda means "Number Forty" according to Xhani. "Forty what?" shouts out someone in the back of our group. Xhani doesn't answer. And the port area alone displays way more than that number of apartment buildings, condominiums and hotels.

When we land and load up another bus, I am grinning as I look around. There is a "Mad Men" 1960s look about the simple, glassy structures and about the pictures on signs. Saranda reminds me of a building set I had as a kid. And just like with my set, a lot of the buildings are unfinished.

"It's a boom town," I say to my seatmate, Alison Appelbe of Vancouver. "Or not. It almost looks like they gave up on them."

"It is the second thing," says Xhani, who has overheard me. We are on our way to the ancient Albanian town of Butrint. In truth, we are at a standstill. It is midmorning rush hour in Saranda. The bus feels like the interior of a pizza oven.

"Somebody ask," says Xhani, "why the buildings empty. Well, I tell you." There is a silence. "It's a bad bank," he explains. "Bad bank."

A woman up front isn't satisfied with the explanation. "Well," says Xhani confidentially, switching off the microphone and softening his tone. "You see, some investment companies have created pyramid fraud. In the 1990s, the pyramid collapse. People are bankrupt. Do you understand?"

We do.

A man with sunglasses is telling Xhani about Bernie Madoff. He seems pleasantly surprised. "We are former communist country," he announces. "It make some people lazy. But not now. Not now." Xhani waves his hand proudly at the trucks and buses that make up the traffic jam just outside.

"Only few years ago, we have 800 cars in all Albania," he adds. "Now our favorite car? Mercedes." I don't see any around, but I take Xhani's word for it.

Finally we are out of the gridlock and winding through fields and farms. "For the cultivation of watermelon," Xhani explains. We pass an enormous lake or inlet that's speckled with wooden posts for farming mussels. It's as long as a Scottish loch and as blue as the sky.

"Well known, well known!" says Xhani about either lake or shellfish.

Just as we pull into Butrint, Xhani fills us in on a few more facts. It's an hour earlier in Albania than in Corfu. The country has a population of about four million. John Belushi and Mother Teresa are of Albanian descent. And, although it's cloudy right now in Butrint, "Each year, Albania has more than 300 days of sun."

Visiting the ruins in Butrint National Park is like getting a private tour of Athens' ancient agora or the Roman forum. A UNESCO World Heritage Site, there are no tickets or lines. In fact there's no one else around. Xhani guides us past the remains of Greek temples from the fourth century B.C. and leftovers from the Roman colony that Julius and Augustus Caesar founded.

It is so eerily quiet at the Lion Gate, a famous doorway with its relief of a lion ripping into part of a bull, that for a second I have the sense that what we're seeing isn't dead. Someone will appear in the doorway, motion us away, or more scary, invite us in.

Sandals are shuffling on gravel. Frogs are peeping from somewhere back in the bushes. A steady humming comes from the mimosa trees above. Xhani motions us to stop and listen.

The hum is just a bass note. Above it is a snappy beat that sounds like it's being tapped out by castanets. On top of that is a kind of chirping that, the more we listen, seems to strain for melody — simple, repetitive — but enough to pass as a tune.

Listen, says Xhani again. "Many kind of insect here!"

The group is eager to move on. "Wait, wait!" urges Xhani. But, passengers are slapping and scratching. A cloud of gnats is rising out of the grass. Something is biting me on the soft side of my foot, just above my flip-flop.

Finally, by waving shirts and jackets we get away from the swarm. "What was that?" asks a woman waving a spray can of all-natural repellent.

"Bugs!" Xhani explains with excitement. "But it is not more than usual," he adds. He seems slightly disappointed.

Our brochure points us to a circular baptistry that's more recent than many of the ruins here, dating from the sixth century A.D. Since I always crave detail in these places I'm glad to see that it's dotted with mosaics. We get to an ancient theater that everyone takes pictures of. Only the Greek gymnasium is disappointing: It is under water. I can see a fish darting between two submerged stones.

Back on the little walkway, we encounter a group of locals sipping coffee. Some are resting on benches. All raise palms to greet us. Why are they here? No one is sure. In an olive grove there is a uniformed guard. He smiles. We smile back. He points the way ahead.

A ray of sun picks out a rim of stones in another ruin that looks worth exploring. But we are late for lunch.

The bus driver races us to a restaurant at the top of a hill. Xhani remains seated, knowing about the corkscrew driveway that spirals us up to the patio and eatery. From up here, we can look down on a stretch of yellow beaches and an aquamarine sea that bleeds to green near the shore.

An Albanian lunch is set out for us on tables with paper cloths and bottles of Tirana beer. The label shows a tower and a two–headed eagle. "That's the national symbol," explains a man in our group who is peeling his off as a souvenir.

First comes a salad that looks Greek with its cucumbers and goat cheese. Some kind of yogurt sauce is delivered along with bread and the freshest humus I've ever tasted. I am feeling full.

"Wait!" says Xhani as two or three people push back from their plates. "It isn't finish. Here come the fish!" We end up with two more courses, plus bowls of fruit for dessert.

"You will come back?" says our waiter in slowly perfect English. He is gravely concerned. "Come tomorrow," he suggests, "for special soup."

I'd like to come back, I say. I'd like to try it.

Someday some of us may return to taste the mussels from the saltwater lake. Or buy the watermelons that are grown in Albania's fields.

Most of all I am hoping to do my part to fill an empty hotel.

On the bus, we see a pair of men saluting us from distant tractors. Another time I would like to meet them. To raise my palm. To shake their hands.

But it cannot be today. Xhani is speaking. Passengers are dozing.

The Flying Dolphin awaits.

Peter Mandel, who lives in Providence, RI, is an author of children's books, including "Jackhammer Sam" (Macmillan) and "Bun, Onion, Burger" (Simon & Schuster). A regular travel contributor to The Washington Post and The Boston Globe, he has written for Harper's, The Wall Street Journal, International Herald Tribune and Los Angeles Times. He has won several Lowell Thomas Travel Journalism awards from the Society of American Travel Writers Foundation.

QUEST FOR THE SACRED SEA SNAIL
Mexico

I'm in a bikini, dangling from the edge of a granite cliff, holding my sarong out to a man in white shorts. It might sound as though I'm auditioning for a gig as an acrobat with Cirque de Soleil, but I'm actually in a secret cove near Puerto Escondido in southern Mexico on a mission to gather natural dye from a sacred sea snail.

I've been invited to participate in the snail expedition by Patrice Perillie, an immigration lawyer and activist who divides her time between Puerto Escondido and New York City. Along with members of the indigenous Mixteco community and Mexican anthropologist Marta Turok, she's actively involved in preserving Oaxaca's *tixinda* snail population.

The dye, derived from the purpura pansa marine snail, has been used to tint elite garments for centuries.

Known as Royal Purple by the ancient Phoenicians and as *tixinda* in Oaxaca, it's an essential color in the *pozahuanco,* a ceremonial Mixteco garment.

Unlike the Mediterranean, where harvesters killed the mollusks to obtain the dye — a practice that led to the snail's extirpation — in Oaxaca the dye is carefully extracted from the snail, thus preserving the tradition for future generations.

Located on Mexico's southern Pacific shore, Puerto Escondido ("hidden port" in Spanish) is home to a small community of ex-pats made up of surfers, New-Age practitioners and budget-minded retirees who are prepared to overlook the beach town's scruffy edges in exchange for plenty of authentic local culture. I'd met Patrice during an event hosted by la Luna Nueva, a group of women that meets monthly for such activities as meditation classes, solstice ceremonies and wellness.

Our circle of participants ranges from teenagers in crop tops to *ancianas,* women with gray hair and in long flowing gowns. I am somewhat in the middle of the group.

Wellness has been much on my mind in the past year. I'd recently emerged from a bout with kidney cancer, and may have looked fine on the outside, but my outlook on life had shifted. Unlike other cancer survivors who vow to live life to the fullest, I had unconsciously slid into a life of caution. I'd once charged through the world, enjoying a successful corporate career, volunteering in Russia, swimming with belugas in Hudson Bay and studying yoga in India. We'd even bought a beach home in Puerto Escondido, planning to retire early. Now, I regularly swap security for adventure. Walking tours replace cycling expeditions; cooking classes for kayaking. It is still a full life by most measures, but a notch or two lower in pace.

When Patrice invited members of la Luna Nueva to participate in a shell-dyeing excursion, I'd readily agreed. I'd be one of the youngest in the group and surely able to keep up, I reason.

Our group departs Puerto Escondido at dawn, headed by mini-van to an undisclosed cove near Huatulco. For untold generations, Mixteco shell-dyers have trekked by foot to this stretch of the Oaxaca Coast, where the *tixinda* snails live within rocky crevasses.

"The location is kept secret in order to prevent poachers or the simply curious from damaging the snail habitat," Patrice explains.

Even with the secrecy, the shell-dyeing tradition has come under threat. In the early 1980s a Japanese corporation, Imperial Purple Inc., nearly stripped the Oaxacan coastline of purpura. The company extracted dye in such large numbers that the snail population was driven to the brink of extinction. Anthropologist Turok and the shell-dyers of Pinotepa successfully petitioned authorities to declare the snail habitat a federally-protected zone, arguing that Mixteco traditions and livelihood were being destroyed.

"Now, only licensed Mixtec dyers are allowed to harvest *tixinda* dye," she says, introducing us to another person in the van. We are accompanied by expert shell-dyer Habacuc Avendano, head of the *Cooperativo de Tintoreros de Pinotepa Don Luis,* some of the last people on earth permitted to harvest the dye from this legendary snail.

"We used to walk for eight days to get here from our village," says Habacuc, who has been harvesting *tixinda* dye since he was 15. "We'd stay on the coast for three months during the harvesting season and then walk back home."

With his mahogany hair, white T-shirt and gym shorts suggesting he is ready to run a quarter-mile sprint, Habacuc looks in his 50s and able to perform the grueling journey. But I do the math and guess he is actually in his mid-70s, decades older than I.

I try to imagine walking for eight days in the blazing heat. The men of Pinotepa de Don Luis would also have been carrying hundreds of skeins of dyed cotton back to the village for the women weavers to use to create the *pozahuanco* garment. It was an epic journey difficult to imagine in modern times.

"How do you get here these days?" I ask.

"We've got the luxury of going by bus or van, but there are so few of us, it's hardly worth hiring transportation."

"How many of you are left?" I ask.

"Just 13," he says. "Even our sons don't have time anymore."

*****

Within an hour, the van makes a turn onto a side road. I guess that we are either in or near Bahias de Huatulco National Park, a mostly wild nature preserve that stretches almost 50 miles along the coast northwest of Huatulco, the manicured resort town created by Fonatur, Mexico's tourism development agency. The preserve is made up of a marine zone, mangroves and dry tropical forest. Hot, dry and thick with vegetation such as cactus, it's not a place you'd want to get lost in.

We then turn onto a gravel road that ends at the launching beach, a patch of sand with a few *palapa* restaurants, a rag-tag collection of fishing skiffs and a crowd of curious kids. We climb into small boats and bounce across sapphire blue waters, passing countless small bays until we turn into a cove flanked by tall rock formations, and pull ashore.

Clutching our scraps of white cloth to be dyed — ranging from sarongs to T-shirts — we set off across the hot sand to a rocky promontory. While walking, Habacuc explains how preserving the life of the snail is an important part of the Mixtec harvesting tradition.

"We only harvest from October until March," he says, hanging his laminated license around his neck.

"And we visit each cove only once each moon cycle. This allows the *tixinda* to regenerate its ink."

Once at the rocks, I stop and stare. What had appeared to be picturesque from afar is actually a jumble of razor-sharp boulders, hammered by waves so ferocious the air is filled with mist.

"Umm…it's steeper than I thought it would be," I say.

"Follow my steps carefully," shouts Habacuc, beckoning me forward. "We only have a few hours before the tide comes in."

The *tixinda* live within the inter-tidal zone, which means shell-dyers – and now I – can only reach the snails during low tide. As Habacuc nimbly scampers over rocks as jagged as dinosaur teeth, I gingerly retrace his steps, placing my feet in crevasses to hold myself upright.

"Is this a *tixinda*? I ask, pointing hopefully to a brown snail in a pool of water. My companions are also calling out possible sightings from their precipitous perches.

"No," he says, with a quick glance, "Keep looking."

Tixinda are elusive. Even with environmental protection, the snail population is diminishing because of illegal poaching and climate change. Finally, Habacuc spots several *tixinda* and, using a rounded stick, gently pries one off the rock, holding it out for me to examine.

The snail's modest appearance surprises me. A nondescript gray, it looks rather unremarkable for a producer of such coveted dye.

"Pass me your cloth," Habacuc says, balancing on the edge of a cliff, snail in hand.

I hold out my white sarong and he delicately squeezes the snail's dye-bearing underbody until a few drops of milky yellow liquid drip onto the cloth. The yellow mucus stored in the snail's hypobranchial gland acts as a narcotic for paralyzing its prey.

"It can take the liquid from 400 snails to dye one skein of cotton," Habacuc explains, pointing to yarn strung loosely around his arm.

He then puts the snail back onto the rock, where it quickly reattaches itself, and repeats the process, snail by snail, dabbing mucus until our cloths are covered in yellow splotches.

"Isn't the dye supposed to be purple?" I wonder, finding it hard to believe royalty would be interested in wearing garments covered in yellow polka dots.

I get my answer minutes later when photooxidization begins doing its magic. The yellow splotches slowly transform into green, then violet and then a deep purple that grows in intensity the longer it is exposed to sunlight.

"There's more here," he shouts from another rocky point, catching my attention with his enthusiasm.

By now, most of my travel companions have returned to the landing beach where they rest under the shade of an almond tree. I continue following Habacuc deeper through the rocks ever closer to the frothing, swelling water. My fears forgotten, I am on a mission to dye my piece of material.

Given the arduous nature of the dyeing process, I begin to wish I'd invested in a more worthy garment to dye. The process, akin to dyeing a tablecloth with a Bingo Dabber, would take hours and hours to complete. My sarong is just a budget piece of cotton purchased at the market. Even though it is modest in value, Habacuc treats it as worthy as a prized *pozahuaco.*

"Why is a *pozahuaco* so important?" I ask, stretching my cloth out for more dye. Although the ones I'd seen were pretty with their rainbow shades of blue and magenta, they were otherwise unadorned — no embroidery or embellishments or anything else that would seem to warrant such a vaulted position in society.

"They wear it upon marriage, throughout their lives for major events and upon death as a death shroud," Habacuc says. "But it's not just the garment that's important. It's as much as about the precision of the four colors used. It must contain deep red (from the cochineal cactus bug), *anil* (indigo), bright red and purple from the *tixinda.*"

*****

Finally, the laborious shell-dyeing process is complete. Arms aching, I return to the beach where our group compares purple creations. It has taken us hours in the hot sun to create our works of art. Unfortunately for the men of Pinotepa like Habacuc, the color purple doesn't fetch a premium in the mainstream market.

"Unless they're educated on the process, most consumers don't appreciate the amount of work involved with natural purple dye and aren't willing to pay a higher price," Patrice says.

"The other challenge is that the remoteness of Pinotepa de Don Luis means there is limited access to clients," she says. She helps support the Pinotepa weaving community by hosting the Dreamweavers Annual Weaving Exhibition and Sale in Puerto Escondido each January. The event features cuisine, music and backstrap loom weaving demonstrations, and has become a major source of income to the cooperative.

As I head back in the van to Puerto Escondido, slightly sunburned and with my shell-dyed sarong in hand, I hope that the Mixteco ancestral traditions and the sacred snail itself will survive for future generations. Given the extent of work involved in harvesting the dye and the disappearing population of *tixinda* snails, it seems unlikely.

Shell-dyeing doesn't appear to be a viable industry. Yet, for Habacuc, that doesn't seem to matter. He is committed to preserving something generations of others have done before him; a pattern carved through time. He draws meaning by doing.

I realize that focused on my shell-dyeing mission, I, too, have found meaning from diving in, not from holding back. I'd forgotten my illness, my fears, my cautions as I'd scrambled over rocks, hanging from precipices with waves rushing at my toes; I'd felt powerful.

Our quest for the sacred snail has turned out to be more than an excursion. For me, it has been a life lesson. Perhaps life shouldn't be defined by its length, but by its passion.

Michele Peterson is an award-winning writer who specializes in travel, cuisine and eco-adventure. She has contributed to more than 100 print and online publications as well as popular book anthologies. She's also the author of the Puerto Escondido Travel Essentials mobile app for IOS and Android. She divides her time between Toronto, Canada, a ramshackle ranch in Guatemala and Puerto Escondido, Mexico, where she plans to learn to surf. Visit her at michelepeterson.com and on Twitter @ATasteForTravel.

THE THIRD LESSON WE LEARNED IN TURKEY
Turkey

"How long is this journey?" Sophia asked. She was 14 and generally mad at Turkey. Today she was mad at the local modesty standards that meant that she was over-dressed for the weather. "I just want to wear short skirts and eat bacon!" my daughter had shouted after 10 days in the country.

"You can," I promised. "Just not for another two and a half months." We were living in İzmir, Turkey's third-largest city, for three months as part of a family year abroad. At Christmas we would move to liberal, pork-loving Spain, but that felt a long way away for Sophia.

Now it was the second week of October, and my kids and I were trying to get to the intercity bus station on the outskirts of town. We had been on the bus for 30 minutes. We were sweaty, cramped and not at all sure that we were headed toward our destination. And Sophia wanted to know how long the journey would be. I answered honestly: "Actually I have no idea. I thought we'd be there by now."

"Seriously? We should just get out and take a cab. I don't even get why we're going out to the bus station in the first place."

I explained again, about the plan hatched by the bus company guy in Avanos. It had sounded unlikely 24 hours ago, and seemed impossible now.

The previous day, we had been in Avanos, a small town in central Anatolia, on the last day of a five-day trip. I had lost a lens for the family camera and was pretty sure I'd left it in the trunk of a car we rented.

Losing a camera lens is not the end of the world, but the timing was bad. I had recently lost the fancy and expensive tripod my husband bought me for my birthday. (Well, actually, my son Sebastian lost it, but you can't blame a 7-year-old when you put him in charge of an expensive item and he leaves it behind in a commuter ferry waiting room). Then, that very day in Avanos, on a whim, I had spent 300 lira hiring a bird watching guide to take me to see flamingos, which was an unexpected expense. If there's anything my spouse hates, it's an unexpected expense. The lens would cost about $100 to replace but that was assuming I could even figure out where to buy one in İzmir. More likely was that we would have to wait until Christmas to get a new one.

So I was highly motivated to retrieve the lens, even though I didn't really believe it was possible.

The young man working at the Turk Car rental office in Avanos did not speak English, so I tried to explain the problem using my phrase-book Turkish.

"Car back of, I lens camera yesterday lose," I tried. Turkish pronunciation is not hard, but the word order and suffixes are very challenging for English speakers. He held up his finger: the universal sign for "Wait a sec, I'm going to try to find someone who knows what the hell you're trying to say."

He brought a friend from the Yeşil Koy (Green Village) bus company office next door, who translated for us.

"Your *lensi* not here," the translator told me. "Probably still in car boot. Your car in Kayseri is. It back come five o'clock."

This was unlucky. Kayseri was an hour away.

"I am going on the bus to Konya now. I can't wait until five o'clock."

"You go to Konya?"

"Yes."

"On Yeşil Koy?"

I had to admit that I was traveling with his company's competitor. He was unfazed.

"Oh. No problem. We send your lens to Konya on our bus. You come to Konya bus station tonight to pick up."

"Oh that is a great idea and so nice of you, but we're not staying in Konya. We're catching the overnight train to İzmir."

"What time your train to İzmir?"

"8 o'clock."

"And what time you get to İzmir?"

"Tomorrow at 9 o'clock." We were taking the overnight train and would arrive home in İzmir for breakfast.

"Hmm." The Yeşil Koy guy went back to his office. I stood there.

He came back with a piece of paper. He was smiling. "OK, the car back come 5 o'clock. We have bus that leave for Nevşehir at 7. We put your *lens*i on bus." He paused to make sure I understood.

I nodded, but couldn't see how putting my camera lens on a bus to Nevşehir would help me in any way.

"Tonight at midnight, we have a bus leaving Nevşehir for İzmir. It arrive İzmir tomorrow 9 o'clock. When you get to İzmir on train, you go bus station, get camera *lensi*."

I didn't know what to think. If this was his way of getting rid of me, it was pretty elaborate. He didn't work for Turk Car. Why was he even involved? Surely he didn't actually expect this plan to work? It depended, first of all, on the lens still being safely in its black leather, thrift-store purse with the broken zipper in the trunk of the rental car when the car was returned to their office that afternoon. It depended on the car being returned before the bus for Nevşehir left at 7 and on someone remembering to get the lens out of the trunk and put it on the bus to Nevşehir, and on that person explaining to the bus driver what it was all about. It depended on the bus to Nevşehir making good time so that the lens could make its connection to the overnight bus to İzmir, and on someone in the Nevşehir office taking responsibility for making the transfer. And all of this was going to happen for free?

But the only possible response was gratitude. I figured there was a greater than 50% chance that this guy was blowing smoke up my ass, but he really did seem sincere. I thanked him and, in a gesture of hopefulness that I didn't feel, I took a piece of paper out of my backpack, wrote my name and email address on it, and "Camera lens in black bag," and held it out to him. He took the small piece of paper from me and smiled again. I said a quick prayer: "Please let this be true."

Belongings are funny. I always want to be Buddhist about them: detached. Our stuff is supposed to work for us, not enslave us. But when I lose something, I am less like a wise-smiling Buddha and more like the shepherd in the parable of the lost sheep. Despite having loads of other sheep, when the shepherd loses one, he goes to all lengths to find that one and return it to the flock. This is pretty much the opposite of detached and this, if I'm being honest, this is how I feel when I lose something. Even a pen. Or a good sock. So, from the moment I handed over that piece of card with my name on it, that lens took up a lot of my mind space. I couldn't stop it from happening. It was my lost sheep.

Back on the İzmir city bus, Sophia merely sighed at this explanation. "I'm so hot!" she said, tugging at her long-sleeved shirt. The long sleeves and pants annoyed her but we both knew that wearing a tank top and shorts would have been a faux pas and drawn uncomfortable attention.

Seeing his opportunity to shine in comparison to his disgruntled sister, Sebastian settled into my lap. "I don't mind Mummy. I want to help you get your lens." I looked out the dirty bus window at the endless gray of the city and looked for clues that would tell me we were getting closer to the bus station.

The first lesson we learned in Turkey was that our usual ways of judging neighborhoods and cities didn't apply here. In Turkey, run-down buildings, graffiti, pot-holed streets, a lack of lighting, and litter are not indicative of a poor, neglected or dangerous place. Our neighborhood in İzmir, on the Aegean Sea, was a typical middle-class neighborhood where everyone had a job, the kids went to school, and crime was rare. Yet by our Canadian standards, it looked rough, even ugly. So we quickly changed our way of seeing.

But even with my adapted Turkey-appropriate out-look, the neighborhoods I was watching out the window of the city bus this hot October afternoon did not feel safe. There were few people on the sidewalks, lots of broken windows, and very few döner stands. I hadn't seen a taxi for 15 minutes.

After 45 minutes there was still no sign of the station. Sophia wasn't the only one getting agitated. A pomaded and perfumed young man sitting behind us was following the bus route with the GPS on his phone. In his other hand he held two Yeşil Koy tickets. He started talking to the man standing next to him — the bus was full to capacity — and pointing at his phone and the tickets. Soon there were half a dozen people giving him advice and he and his girlfriend were moving to the exit door.

"If they're getting off," I thought, "that means this bus isn't going to the station."

Advice was being shouted at the couple from all over the bus. I heard the word "taxi" repeated several times. I couldn't decide whether I should get out with them and try to share a taxi or continue to wait it out on the bus. I wished my Turkish was better, or that I was braver. I watched the young couple disembark, then quickly hail a taxi and zoom off.

"Lucky for us we aren't in a hurry!" I said to the kids. "Otherwise we'd have to pay for a taxi, like those guys." I played it cool for the kids' sake, but my real fear wasn't that the bus was taking too long, but that it was taking us too far.

After an hour we were far from anything we'd seen before. Greater İzmir has a population of 8 million and spreads out far to the east, the side that isn't bordered by the Aegean. I told the kids that the worst-case scenario was that we rode the bus in a big loop and ended up back downtown. It wasn't fun, but we weren't in danger. "Bus routes always go back to where they started," I said. But was this really true? For all I knew, this bus would finish its route 50 kilometers from downtown İzmir and just stop there. Everyone would get off and there would be no taxis and we would be completely lost in a dangerous neighborhood and unable to get help.

We would get mugged and raped. Sebastian, whom every single Turkish person adored, would be taken into a new family and raised as one of them. Sophia and I would have our bloody bodies tossed into a field somewhere to be found weeks later by a shepherd.

I thought these things while I kept smiling and pointing things out to the kids as if we were on a sightseeing tour. "Oh look there's another one of those Sebastiani salons! I didn't know you owned so many, Sebastian! And ooooh, that looks like a good döner stand. Maybe we'll come back here with Daddy later and try it out."

I was reading every sign I saw and finally I saw one that said "Otobus Terminali" with an arrow pointing in the direction we were going. "Look look! Sophia! Look! The bus station! There's a sign! We're going in the right direction."

"Great," she said, not looking. "This bus stinks," she added. I couldn't disagree there. Compared to the smells of all the bodies squashed together inside the bus, the wafts of diesel and cigarette smoke that came through the windows from time to time were heaven-sent.

At the next stop, a lot of people got off. Finally I could move to the front of the bus to talk to the driver. "Otobus terminali?" I asked. He answered in a string of Turkish of which I only caught one word: "Evet". Yes. Also, he was smiling. So I figured we were good.

Ten minutes later, we got off the bus, crossed a road, and we were at the bus station. All this, I thought, for a lens that is likely in a pawn shop hundreds of kilometers away in Kayseri by now.

We entered the cool, spacious bus terminal, found the Yeşil Koy desk, and asked "*Ingilizce konuşuyor musunuz*?" Do you speak English?

They found someone who did, and I explained why I was there. "Do you have your ticket?" he asked.

"No, because I didn't take a bus. I took a train. But my lens was supposed to come on the bus this morning from Nevşehir."

"You took a train from Nevşehir?" he asked, confusion on his face. There is no train from Nevşehir.

"No I took a train from Konya but my lens was coming from Avanos. To Nevşehir last night and then to İzmir this morning. If they found it, I mean. I don't know if they did. Did you get a lens in a black bag today?"

There were five men wearing green Yeşil Koy sweaters and suddenly they were all on the case. Three were on the phone. The other two were looking at bus schedules from central Anatolia. All I could think was "What the hell am I doing here? What incentive could any of

these people have for helping me? I'm not even their cus-
tomer."

I had recovered from the anxiety of the bus ride and
was starting to feel sad about my lost sheep again.

After several minutes, an older man with bushy black
eyebrows and a kind smile looked over at me and said
"*Çay?*"

The second lesson we learned in Turkey was that
nothing happens without *çay*. Tea.

Whether you're eating breakfast, buying shoes, riding
the ferry or negotiating a rental agreement, you always
drink çay in Turkey. Made from leaves grown on the
Black Sea, Turkish tea is typically overbrewed, then watered down to the taste of the drinker, and served in a
small, tulip-shaped glass with a cube or two of sugar on
a little saucer. It can be an acquired taste for Westerners
used to taking their tea with milk but our family had gotten hooked on it quickly, and we drank it several times a
day, at home and out. We first learned how consoling a
glass of Turkish tea could be after the incident with the
tripod in the ferry waiting room. Sebastian and I both
drank tea on the ferry afterward and felt better.

Back at the bus station, I wondered if the offer of tea
wasn't a prelude to the revelation that my lens was lost
forever, but it didn't really matter. The lens was either
coming or it wasn't. We might as well drink tea.

"*Evet, teşekkür ederim.*" I said. Yes, thank you. The
man gestured at us to meet him around the back of the
office, where the buses came. We sat on a bench and he

handed us hot, bitter Turkish tea in Styrofoam cups. I took a sip and the tea worked its magic. I saw that things could have been much worse. I was going to hear in a couple minutes that they didn't know what I was talking about, that no lens had come from Avanos, that they don't courier lost items for free to people who aren't even their customers, but at least they were kind.

Another older man from the staff came over and started fooling around with Sebastian, stealing his hat and putting it on his own head. Sebastian smiled.

We finished our tea. I was calm. We were safe. I could buy a new lens. I had tried my best to retrieve it, so my spouse could not be too mad at me. If he was, I would tell him how lucky he was that we weren't lying bloodied in a field. But first I had to wait for this little drama to wrap up. It seemed that none of the staff of Yeşil Koy wanted to be the ones to tell me the bad news. I wondered how to get a status report without appearing ungrateful or rude. The bottom line was that I was searching for property that I had lost through my own carelessness. I was also cognizant of the fact that the property I was trying to retrieve was probably something that would never be affordable to anyone who worked as counter staff for Yeşil Koy.

And then from across the parking lot appeared a mirage. A young man walking toward me in a Yeşil Koy sweater. In his left hand was a small black purse with a broken zipper.

"Oh my God," I said. "That's my purse." I put down my empty paper cup and stood up. My mouth was open and I held my hands out, open to heaven like a Baptist during worship time.

"Don't cry Mummy," Sophia warned. On the handle of the purse was stapled the piece of paper I had handed to the man in Avanos. Inside was my *lensi*.

I felt overwhelmed with gratitude for the kindness of the people who had worked this small miracle. It was just a lens, yes, but that was the point. It was just a lens, and I was just a visiting foreigner, and yet they'd made such efforts to restore it to me, and it had all worked just as the young translator in Avanos had said it would. I shook hands with each of the green-sweatered men, who were standing around beaming, clearly pleased at the turn of events, and repeated "*Çok çok teşekkür ederim*!" Thank you very, very much.

We caught a cab back home. Sophia rolled down the cab's window and stuck her head out. The driver sped along the large highway connector that went over and around the traffic-snarled neighborhoods that the bus had trudged through so slowly. Very soon we were in familiar territory, and the smell coming through the window was of street food and the sea.

The third lesson we learned in Turkey was that nothing can go wrong in Turkey. Getting back my lens was the first, but not the last time, that something that seemed incredibly unlikely to happen just went ahead and happened anyway. We used the phrase as a mantra when it seemed like something might go wrong. "Did that waiter understand our order?" Of course he did, because nothing can go wrong in Turkey. "We're late for the bus. If we run and wave, will the driver skid to a stop and let us on?" Yes, because nothing can go wrong in Turkey. And the most often asked question in my mind: "Are we safe?" Definitely. We're in Turkey.

Rebeca Dunn-Krahn is a mother, software developer and traveler who enjoys reading, eating and unexpected adventures. She lives in Victoria, BC, Canada.

BLOWING THE BLUES WITH THE BATWA
Uganda

"*Wakoze Kuza*," says Batwa pygmy Chief "Steve" Var-aheegwan, welcoming us to his tribal village in the Virunga Mountains of Uganda. Herbert, the vivacious Ugandan liaison, translates his welcome for me.

The entire Batwa tribe of about 75 men, women and children stare, and I try not to show my surprise at their relatively normal height. These people are not the pygmies I had imagined. Herbert later explains that they have intermarried with other tribes.

I've just huffed and puffed two hours up an unending hill at an altitude of 8,500 feet to meet this indigenous Ugandan tribe, a cultural visit that the safari lodge where I'm staying, Mount Gahinga Lodge, offers to Muzungus (as we foreigners are called by the Ugandans).

The new Batwa cultural program was created by Volcanoes Safaris Partnership Trust to help the Batwa revive their traditions so their history and culture could be better understood by the local communities and by the younger Batwa generation.

The Trust has built a Batwa Heritage Site to show how the tribe used to live in the forest. It's also constructed a cultural center where the Batwa women learn to sew and make straw baskets; each week they do a cultural singing and drumming performance, which I am hoping to see shortly, along with the other four Mount Gahinga Lodge guests who've hiked up the mountain with me.

We are still catching our breath when the chief explains that the tribe will instead perform the dance ceremony tomorrow for the entire community. He offers us a tour of the round huts made from branches and twigs and with thatched roofs.

Up until 1992, the Batwa lived in the forest and made their living hunting, foraging for vegetables and harvesting honey; then the government evicted them and turned their land into a national park. Now they live as squatters in these drafty huts with no water or electricity or any other necessities we're used to in the west. Inside, the sparse walls are blackened from cooking. There are no beds, no furniture, just a couple of burned pots and a sleeping space on the bare ground.

As we exit the cramped hut, some children crowd around us, including a little boy wearing a man's shirt that comes down to his ankles. A girl wearing a torn yellow dress touches my hand and giggles. Both males and females of all ages wear their hair cropped short, and the only way you can tell who's who is that the girls wear thread worn skirts. They might be poor, but they look healthy and their smiles are real.

Batwa children don't go to school but often help their parents who eke out a living working in the fields and performing cultural visits. Tomorrow's dance ceremony, for which they will receive a small sum, helps pay for salt, soap, sheep and goats.

While the dance ceremony helps keep their cultural traditions alive, they also abandoned some customs after leaving the forest, such as praying to their gods. They've been introduced to other religions, and many, such as Chief Steve, have adopted Christian names. Herbert translates as one of the older men tells me, "Life in the forest was good. We never lacked for anything; we had food, we had medicinal herbs and meat, we had clean water, but now have to buy our water. Life was not monetary in the forest. When we left the forest, our first challenge was land."

At first, he tells us, other tribes received them because they provided cheap labor, but now it's difficult for the Batwa because the population has increased and there are few jobs.

It's time for a photo op, and the four of us take turns posing with the tribe. Then Herbert announces we're leaving. It's not as though going back down will be a hardship — there are gigantic extinct volcanoes in every direction, children waving as they herd goats, women carrying huge bundles of branches on their heads, and men digging in the fields with hoes — the images are worth the steep climb back down, but I'm not ready to leave so soon.

Before the trip, I had asked the Hohner Company to donate 30 pink plastic Hohner harmonicas, as I knew they'd be perfect gifts for the Batwa children. But I do a quick count and realize there are at least 50 kids. How do I decide which ones should get a harmonica?

Suddenly I have an idea. I pull out my own harmonica from my pocket and hold it up. They look curiously, never having seen one, the usual reaction I get when I show people from foreign cultures my little pocket-sized 10-hole instrument.

I began to play harmonica a few years ago, primarily to communicate in tongues I didn't speak. Music is the universal language, a perfect icebreaker wherever I am. I clap my hands in a rhythm and pantomime that the Batwa should clap with me. Tentatively, they put their hands together.

I play a boogie-woogie and, by the third bar, they're clapping loud, swaying and tapping their feet on the ground. When I finish, they break out into huge smiles and applaud. I only wish I had enough pink harmonicas for everyone.

After lunch the next day, I'm in my room staring at the pouring rain outside. I assume the Batwa performance has been canceled, but suddenly I hear the sound of pounding drums. I grab my jacket and backpack of harmonicas and run to the front lawn of the lodge.

About 100 people from the local community plus the entire Batwa tribe have gathered to watch 16 Batwa performers, a few of whom I recognize from yesterday's visit, now dressed in identical bright saffron-colored *pareas,* singing, dancing and playing drums. Two women have babies strapped to their backs and a third breast-feeds her infant strapped to her torso as she pounds out a rhythm on the drum.

Five Batwa dancers snake their way in front of the singers and move on the wet grass. Chief Steve, shell necklaces crisscrossed on his bare torso and a shell headband on his forehead, leads the troop. The beat is infectious, the singing intoxicating. I shoot photos, then put my camera in my backpack and clap.

They play for a half-hour or more, and when they finally stop I pull one of the pink plastic harmonicas from my backpack. They begin to clap out a rhythm anticipating I will play, but I have something else in mind: I take the pink harmonicas from my backpack and hand them out one by one to the performers. I pantomime that they should bring the harmonica to their lips and blow.

"Inhale, and then exhale," I tell them. They don't understand what I mean so Herbert, who is at my side shielding me with a giant umbrella, translates.

I breathe in, making the sound of a chord, and breathe out, producing a second chord. The performers immediately get it, creating a rhythm as powerful as the drums. We blow in and out together on the two chords, tapping our feet, the drums still pounding. I move from performer to performer, bringing my face close to theirs, improvising a melody line as they breathe in and out, creating the rhythm.

Herbert is still following me around with the giant umbrella and I feel ridiculous, like British royalty, so I hand him a pink harmonica and tell him to drop the umbrella and play. His eyes light up as he folds up the umbrella, joins the performers and happily blows away. The entire community is clapping.

Two village elders come dancing up to us. Herbert stops playing long enough to tell me to give them each a harmonica. They, too, join us. One of them doesn't even use his hands, but blows in and out, the instrument firmly planted between his lips. When the crowd sees me giving out pink harmonicas, they race up and hold out their hands expectantly.

I pull the rest from my backpack but run out quickly, so I kneel down and play at eye level for the kids who didn't get one. And in the pouring rain in this remote Ugandan village beneath the volcanoes, we joyously send our music to the universe and stop only when we are completely exhausted.

The next morning as I'm climbing into the Jeep to head for the airport, I hear the distant sound of a harmonica, the same riff I taught the Batwa yesterday.

I follow the sound up a nearby trail where a barefoot 8-year-old boy is playing his pink plastic harmonica. He stops when he sees me, but I encourage him to keep going. He plays, and when he's finished I applaud, then put my palms together and bow to him. He grins, holds up the harmonica and bows back.

Margie Goldsmith, winner of 31 writing awards including the prestigious Gold Lowell Thomas Award, writes regularly for Black Card Mag, Elite Traveler, Business Jet Traveler, Robb Report and Global Business Travel, among others. In her spare time she practices mixed martial arts and plays blues harmonica.

THE THREE WISE MEN
USA

Some people have the courage to acknowledge their dreams and go after them, just like that. Others need a little push. Or, in my case, a big push.

I had always been in love with words and travel. I could read all day and had no problem writing several essays a week. Yet I never went abroad for longer than eight days until I was 25 and I never volunteered to write for our university's paper, or anything else for that matter.

I was afraid. Afraid to fail, to discover that I had no talent for the things I loved so much.

In the summer of 2012, however, things changed. I had decided to combine my two passions into a project of my own: a travel blog. On top of that I was leaving on a two-week trip with a friend to Los Angeles and Las Vegas. The blog was only a couple of weeks old and I was weak in the knees when I left on that trip, but I had taken a first step.

Little did I know that it would be three strangers who'd set me free to run.

The substitute family

You know how in movies or books the protagonist often needs a medium to get a certain tool to work? Well, my "medium" was my friend Sylvie. She is as open and social as they come and it quickly became clear that ignoring strangers wasn't an option when traveling with her.

It started on the plane to LAX. We'd gotten seats by the plane's emergency exit, and the passenger sitting next to us asked jokingly whether we'd be able to get the door open if necessary. Sylvie immediately replied, and soon we were chatting away with Michael. We shared our plans for Los Angeles with him and were happy when he said we'd drafted a nice itinerary.

"Will you also visit Laguna Beach?" We wouldn't.

Laguna Beach was more than an hour's drive from where we were staying and we hadn't intended to leave Los Angeles, except to go to Las Vegas for two days. Yet Michael absolutely wanted us to see his hometown. He gave us the number of his son Matt, who lives in New York but was visiting California and would happily guide us around Laguna Beach. At least that's what his father said. Nervous about contacting a guy we didn't know, we texted Matt during our layover at JFK airport and, to my surprise, he agreed to meet us the next day.

Were we really going to spend the day with someone we'd never even met?

After our first night in LA, Matt arrived at our hostel and drove us to Laguna Beach. He told us about himself and laughed when he learned we didn't know what "surf punk" was.

In Laguna, he showed us around and introduced us to his friends. Afterward, he took us to his parents' place, where we saw Michael again and met his wife. Home-made appetizers and cold drinks were served instantly — it was like we were visiting old friends. We could even use their shower to freshen up.

When Matt took us out for dinner that night, we asked how we could ever repay him and his family. All that he asked was that we would do the same for him if ever he should visit Belgium, where I'm from.

We couldn't have started our trip in a better way. We had met a family that had welcomed us into their home, showed us their city and made sure we'd leave with a positive memory of Laguna Beach.

They also had set the tone for the rest of our trip, because that night I decided to be more open toward strangers.

For the next two weeks I started conversations with more people that I didn't know than I had an entire year before back home. I learned to step away from the schedule I'd made for our trip and grasp the chance of doing something new whenever it presented itself.

Of course, Sylvie also had a big hand in this change, but I'm pretty sure it was the experience with Michael's family that really opened me up. It was as if I needed to step out of my comfort zone just once to expand it tremendously.

The guy who booked us a hotel room

If Michael and his family boosted my confidence, then Charles made sure I didn't leave that feeling in LA when I headed back home.

We met Charles on our flight back from Las Vegas, where we'd spent two days before flying home from LAX. I knew he'd spotted us when we'd entered the plane and took our seats in the row behind him, but he fell asleep as soon as we left the ground.

Meanwhile, Sylvie and I had struck up a conversation with a woman on the plane who lived and worked in Las Vegas. We were still talking with her when we landed and Charles woke up.

His head turned toward us and we could tell he was following our conversation, but he didn't join in. I remember thinking how I used to be just like that only two weeks earlier — how I used to notice other people talking but never dared join the conversation or simply introduce myself.

Charles didn't look like he was shy, though, so when we saw him again after having picked up our luggage Sylvie called out to him.

"Hi again!"

That's all it took, and after we'd gotten the mandatory "Where are you from? Where are you going?" out of the way, he asked what we had planned for our last night in the city.

"We're just spending the night at a motel near the airport, as we're flying home early tomorrow morning."

He couldn't believe what he was hearing. Was that how we were spending our last night in Los Angeles? We should at least go out to dinner with him.

Two weeks earlier I would never have gotten in a car with a man I'd met only 5 minutes ago, but that was then, and so we boarded the airport shuttle to the parking lot.

On our way there Charles made a call. We heard him ask for a room, and then recited some numbers.

He'd booked us a room at the Sheraton.

"What!?"

You can imagine we had more than a few alarm bells going off, so we sent his details to some friends in case something went wrong. We were open-minded and wanted to take a chance, but we weren't foolish.

Having reached a new state of excitement (dinner *and* a fancy hotel room) we let Charles drive us to Manhattan Beach, where he bought us dinner and drinks.

"Why are you doing this for us?"

He explained that he'd heard us strike up a conversation with the woman next to us on the plane, and that he envied us because he would never start talking to a stranger. And, since he didn't have any plans that night, going out with us had made his evening more fun.

Flattery, but we didn't protest.

When it was time to head to our hotel, Charles let Sylvie drive us in his Jeep. This raised him yet to another level of cool, but at the same time we couldn't help but wonder what would happen next.

This complete stranger had booked and paid a hotel room for us, and had bought us dinner and drinks. What do *you* think happened when we got to the hotel?

Well, it didn't.

Charles said goodbye to us in the lobby, politely and even a bit reserved. There were no hints, no attempts, nothing suggestive. We had trusted a stranger and he had repaid us with nothing but respect.

While Charles had just wanted to show us a good time on our last night in LA, he had done so much more for me. He confirmed my experience in Laguna Beach and proved that we didn't just get lucky there, that kind strangers are everywhere. You just have to be willing to see them.

The "go for it" guy

So, that's where it ends, right? We were flying home. Who else were we going to meet? Well, just as we met

Michael on the plane to LA, I ended up next to Charlton on my flight from LAX to JFK. (Sylvie was taking a flight later.)

Charlton's family was originally from Italy, but had moved to the States when he was a boy. He'd married an American woman and together they had a bunch of kids.

After we had covered the basic questions, Charlton asked how I'd liked LA. I knew it sounded cliché but told him I'd really felt as if anything was possible there. Maybe this feeling came partly from the positive encounters I'd had, but there was definitely something else as well. Some kind of positive vibe that seemed to motivate people and keep them going, chin up.

I waited for Charlton to start laughing, but he didn't. He said he knew what I meant and that he'd experienced it too. We concluded that there is an American "live-the-dream" attitude that contrasts heavily with the soberness throughout Europe.

Most European countries advocate walking in line, being normal, having "reasonable" dreams. Whenever someone wants to do something a little bit out of the ordinary, reactions usually range from a smug laugh to "You'll never be able to do that" and "You're crazy."

Not so in America, and especially not so in Los Angeles.

Charlton told me that he used to be really "European" about big dreams, until his wife and daughter proved him wrong. Charlton's daughter loves to act. She performed in school plays and took extra acting classes. It was all pretty amateurish until one day she came home and told her parents that she wanted to be on television and in movies. Charlton laughed. He knew how many people move to LA to pursue a career in show business and how few of them actually succeed. He didn't want to nurture his daughter's "crazy dreams."

His wife, however, simply said "OK" and went on a hunt for auditions. A few weeks later their daughter got to act in a commercial and in a TV show episode. The big dreams had won.

I'll never forget this story. I'll never forget how a stranger opened up to me and told me he'd had the wrong attitude, hadn't believed in big dreams and then was converted. I'll never forget how he converted me.

Three wise men

Those men that I met on my trip to Los Angeles – Michael, Charles, Charlton – are my three wise men. They showed me to open up, be confident and have faith, not faith in some higher abstract being, but in people — the stranger next to me on the plane, the stranger waiting in line in front of me at the coffee shop, and the stranger passing me on the street.

And maybe even more important, they've showed me to have faith in myself.

Sofie Couwenbergh is a freelance writer and founder of the travel blog Wonderful Wanderings. From researching and writing for the Belgian press agency Belga, she switched to reporting on the many places her wanderlust takes her.

C. LILL AHRENS

A SIMPLE SYSTEM
Korea

I awoke thinking the mountain was on fire, confused for a moment by the street lamp that transformed our frosted window into a giant yellow nightlight. I could read my watch by it: 4 a.m. Icy gusts rattled the window pane, the probable cause of my wakening. For the past week the wind had blasted down the mountain, chilling us from the ankles up. Our Korean apartment was heated by water pipes embedded in the concrete floor. We would have turned up the heat, but possessed neither thermostat nor furnace room key.

Shivering, I realized the covers had slipped from our sleeping mat. As I pulled the floor-warmed polyester comforter back onto the polyester sheets, static electricity crackled in the bedding, but Paul slept undisturbed. I ducked under the covers to watch the sparks in the dark.

A hinge creaked. I held my breath listening, more curious than concerned; our front door opened with a distinctive scrape. The creaking hinge probably belonged to the door of our furnace room on the landing. I wondered why anyone would be out there at 4 a.m., but was reluctant to leave my warm bed to find out.

Metal clanked on metal. Curiosity won. I pulled on my robe and slippers and cracked open the front door. Our landing was sheltered from the wind, but the air was tear-freezing cold. The night smelled like wood smoke and ice. Heat and light beckoned from the furnace room door a few feet away. I stepped across the landing for my first glimpse inside.

Engrossed in her task, her delicate profile lit by a bare bulb, our landlady, Mrs. Han, seemed unaware of my arrival. Somehow elegant in a black sweatsuit, she stood in front of a cast-iron, waist-high furnace unlike any I'd ever seen. It had a solid front and sides, and three lids in a row on top. Hissing contentedly, it warmed me like a campfire, leaving my backside to freeze.

Mrs. Han gripped the handles of arm-length fire tongs with both hands, hooked the handle of the left lid and slid it aside. Then, with movements sure and graceful, she lowered the fire tongs straight down into the furnace, squeezed the handles together, and began to lift something straight up. What slowly emerged was a glowing red cylinder — a jumbo coal briquette, or "brique" — the size and shape of a gallon paint can. It had eight holes drilled in its top for the tongs to grip and air to circulate.

Mrs. Han kept lifting it until her arms extended high above her head, and the brique cleared the top of the furnace. Her face reflected red from the brique and glistened from the heat. She lowered the brique onto the concrete floor, where it sizzled a safe distance from her pink-plastic-slippered feet. Blue fire licked up the holes from deep within.

Gazing into the lambent flames, I savored the woodsy smell, realizing that the ever-present scent in the air was not wood smoke but burning coal.

I remembered the day two weeks ago, when Paul and I first saw our apartment. Our translator, Miss Yu, had told us, "Mrs. Han will start furnace." It hadn't occurred to me the furnace might be coal. I never dreamed that starting it meant maintaining it too. I had a strong feeling that if we were Mrs. Han's usual Korean tenants rather than Americans, she would not be stoking it for us.

With a flash of guilt and dismay I realized Mrs. Han had been stoking it for two weeks, without any appreciation from us. She had her own furnace to tend. We shouldn't add to her burden. Paul worked long hours, but expatriate spouses weren't allowed to hold jobs, so I had practically nothing to do. The thought of making Mrs. Han's life easier warmed me inside, but more to the point — I wanted to play with the fire. I missed our fireplace in Colorado. And with me in charge of the heat, Paul and I could be warmer. Though my coal-stoking experience was limited to backyard barbecues, I figured: how hard could this be?

Mrs. Han guided the tongs down the hole in the furnace again, and this time lifted out a gray burned-out brique of the same size and shape. She set it on the floor, gripped the still-burning brique, and returned it to the furnace. Then she reached the tongs into the shadows behind her and retrieved a new brique, glossy black. She lowered it into the furnace, then slid closed the lid.

The simplicity of the system enchanted me. Before the top brique burned out it was switched to the bottom position, where it passed the torch to the new one on top of it. A chain reaction. Perpetual fire. Eternal flame.

Hoping not to startle Mrs. Han, I knocked softly on the door frame. She turned and smiled up at me, as if she'd known I was there all along. A key dangled from her necklace made of twine. She bowed slightly, the tongs pressed between her palms like prayer sticks.

When she straightened, I put my hand on the tong handles. With my other hand I pointed to myself and to the furnace, showing I wanted to take over. Smiling, she shook her head no.

I couldn't tell if her refusal was because stoking was a landlady's job, or because I was American and therefore presumed incompetent. I tried to reassure her and explain my intent at the same time by tugging slightly on the tongs, grinning determinedly. Still smiling, she kept hold. Smiling back, I began a steady pull.

Cocking an eyebrow at me in wonder or skepticism, she let go. I hugged the tongs to my chest and bowed to show I intended to take over for good. She shrugged a good-natured "OK."

That settled, Mrs. Han became all business. She pointed to the pipes near the floor that led from the furnace to the water heater, and from the water heater into the wall of the house. I nodded my understanding; she'd given me a quick lesson on how the floors were heated. She pointed to the middle and right lids on the furnace, and mimed lifting briques in and out. I nodded; those still needed to be stoked.

She pointed to three tiny air vents near the floor on the front of the furnace, one below each lid. They were opened just a hair. I nodded; the vents could be adjusted to allow more air into the furnace. I knew that the more air, the hotter the furnace would burn — and the warmer my home would be.

She tapped her fingertip on the 10 of her wristwatch. I nodded, though I wasn't sure if she meant stoke the furnace again at 10 a.m. or 10 p.m.

10 p.m. made more sense, as she could have stoked every night without our knowledge. But I'd check it at 10 a.m. to be safe. She lifted the necklace from her neck and, on tip-toe, placed it over my head. I closed my hand on the key. We bowed. She trotted down the concrete steps to her apartment.

The fire was all mine.

I switched off the bare bulb, too harsh for this soft hour, and took her place before the furnace. I listened to the contented *shhhhhhhhhhh* as my eyes adjusted to the vents' faint orange glow. Then, with tongs more awkward than she'd made them look, I slid aside the center lid. Instantly I was mesmerized by the blue flames dancing in and around a glowing red brique sitting in a white-hot shaft.

The furnace was made of fire brick sheathed in cast-iron, like a pottery kiln with three chambers. The chambers, or shafts, were barely wider in diameter than the briques.

My face tingled from the intense heat. I gripped the tong handles with both hands, aimed down the shaft, stabbed the burning brique through two of its holes, squeezed and began to lift what felt like a concrete block. It weighed much more than Mrs. Han's graceful movements had led me to believe. Raising it without knocking it against the shaft walls, then lowering it to the floor without dropping it or setting my robe on fire, took muscles I didn't know I had. I released it on the floor, far from the hem of my robe. Hearing the sizzle on the concrete, I smiled.

I lowered the tongs into the shaft again and removed the much lighter, burned-out brique. Gazing spellbound into the white-hot shaft, I spotted another dead brique at the bottom. Mrs. Han hadn't removed it, so neither did I. I placed the burning brique on top of it, set a new one on top of that and slid closed the lid. I repeated the procedure for the third and last shaft.

Then, to make our apartment warmer, I opened the vents to half way, about a quarter inch.

Reluctantly I left the warm furnace room, quickly locked the door, sprinted into the apartment and spooned in beside Paul, my human furnace. I drifted into sleep, basking in the anticipated warmth of his appreciation.

I awoke shivering, shortly before Paul's 7 a.m. alarm. The comforter had slipped off again. Paul's arm lay across my chest, his knee on my stomach. My teeth were chattering like the window pane. I pulled the crackling comforter over us. But it was cold.

I placed my palm on the floor. Stone cold.

Watching our breath blow away like smoke, I wished I were dreaming.

I canceled the alarm before it buzzed, disentangled myself from Paul without waking him, pulled on my clothes and parka and hustled outside. When I opened the furnace room door, no heat welcomed me. No reassuring hiss. I grabbed the tongs and shoved the lids aside. The shafts were dark. I lifted out each brique, hoping to find some spark of life. But they were dead. All dead.

Three hours after being entrusted with it, I had killed Mrs. Han's eternal flame.

Paul and I breakfasted in our hats and coats, the gas stove turned on high.

"My secretary speaks Korean," Paul said, "I'll ask her to call Mrs. Han."

"No! I mean, no need to trouble Mrs. Han. I'll ask Miss Yu how to start it."

Paul left for work. I phoned Miss Yu.

"You need fire starter," she said. "General store."

Of course, like a barbecue. I found "lighter fluid" in my *Berlitz Korean for Travelers*, practiced the Korean pronunciation, and set off for the little general store.

It seemed there was always a different family member keeping shop. Today's clerk looked about 12.

"*Rah ee toh kee room*?" I said, and showed him "lighter fluid" in my *Berlitz.*

He held out a disposable cigarette lighter from the counter display. I shook my head "no," pointed to a plastic bucket full of fire tongs, then to "lighter fluid" again.

"Ah!" He laughed. "*Zoot!*"

"Zoot?"

From a plastic bucket next to the coal tongs, he retrieved what looked like a big hockey puck. Made of coal, it was the same diameter as a brique, with the same holes drilled through it. He took a match from his pocket, pretended to light it and touched it to the puck. "*Zoot!*" he laughed, and threw his hands in the air as if to say "problem solved."

I smiled with relief, and nodded my understanding. A *zoot* was similar to the wax and wood fire-starters I'd used in fireplaces, but made from coal and probably lighter fluid. It could be lit with a match and would burn long and steady enough to light a brique.

I bought several *zoots* and a box of matches. I also bought a plastic bucket, since he had no metal ones, to cart the dead briques down to the trash.

In the furnace room, I took up the tongs, stabbed a *zoot* through two of its holes, and rested it on the furnace while I thought about how to proceed. The shafts were about 2 feet deep. If I put the unlit *zoot* into the shaft, it would be difficult to reach down and light it without the match burning my fingers. But the tongs didn't close tight enough to hold a match. I decided to light the *zoot* first, then lower it into the shaft.

Holding a lighted match at arm's length, I touched it to the *zoot*. With a split-second chain-reaction of sparks, *"zzzzzzzzZZZZOOT!!!"* it burst into flames. Black acrid smoke filled the room. I couldn't see, couldn't breathe, dropped the *zoot* and stumbled out the door.

Billowing smoke, the *zoot* wobbled out after me.

I dashed into the apartment and slammed the door, coughing, eyes watering, thankful the building was made of bricks and concrete.

When the smoke cleared and the *zoot* had calmed to a smolder, I retrieved it with the tongs. I placed it at the bottom of the first shaft. Recalling the buzzing sparks that had proceeded its explosion, I theorized that *zoot*s were impregnated with gun powder.

My next attempt went more smoothly. I placed an unlit *zoot* in the second shaft, tossed in a lighted match, ran into the house and stayed there until the smoke dissipated. I repeated for the third and last shaft, then added new briques to each one. Nothing to it.

And once the briques were lit, getting the furnace hot again was simple as well. Knowing that the more air the fire got the sooner our floors would warm, I opened the vents all the way (a half-inch) and fed the furnace every two hours, day and night, like a famished newborn. Meanwhile, Paul and I lived in our coats and soaked up the heat at the neighborhood bathhouse.

After two nights I was exhausted from lack of sleep and the floors were only a tad less cold. Paul offered to help with the night feedings but I turned him down; he needed all his strength for his job. He asked if I wanted Mrs. Han to resume control, and again I refused. I had broken it; I would fix it. I couldn't let down America.

Four days after restarting the furnace, I lay spread-eagled on my tummy, hugging the warm floor in celebration. I had learned a lot that week. I'd learned that once my furnace was hot it took hours to heat the water tank, and once the water was hot, it took even longer for the pipes to heat the floor. I'd learned that briques were called *yontan,* where to find the closest *yontan* shop, that the minimum order was 200, and that luckily they only cost about a quarter each. I'd learned that if you don't wait long enough before putting dead *yontan* in the bucket, you melt the bucket.

But I hadn't learned my lesson.

With the vents reset at Mrs. Han's "just a hair," the furnace needed to be stoked every six hours — how she had tended it for two weeks without my knowledge was a mystery. And the frigid wind wouldn't cease. I wanted the furnace to burn faster during the day for more warmth, and slower at night so I could get eight hours of unbroken sleep. I figured it was simply a matter of fine-tuning the air vents. However, having learned from experience, I began my warming experiment by setting the vents a single hair's breadth beyond "just a hair," and kept close watch on the burning *yontan.*

As it turned out, any vent position other than "all the way" or "just a hair" made the burn rate unpredictable, put the shafts out of sync, and soon I was practically living in the furnace room, feeding each shaft at a different time like newborn triplets.

A few nights later, seriously sleep deprived, the truckload of new *yontan* stacked blackly behind me, I slumped against the furnace room wall. Gathering the strength to feed the hungry second shaft, I stared into the rambunctious flames of the first, noting the similarity to the fires of hell. Somehow I had to get these babies on a schedule.

I remembered Mrs. Han tapping her finger on the 10 of her watch. I recalled finding her at 4 a.m., standing before the furnace as if it were an altar. The answer came to me: *Enough already with the Yankee "ingenuity."*

I sighed, took up the tongs, and started over. One by one, except for the dead one at the bottom of each shaft, I lifted all the *yontan* — all in various stages of fiery consumption — up and out of the furnace and, for lack of space, shuttled them out of the furnace room to the end of the frigid landing.

Next, still using the tongs, I lowered an unlit *zoot* into the first shaft — careful not to touch it to the white-hot sides and trigger a premature explosion — and noted the practicality of having a dead *yontan* in the bottom to serve as a *zoot* platform. I placed a *zoot* in each of the other shafts. I lit three matches in close succession, tossed one into each shaft, leapt out the door and slammed it behind me just as "*zzzzzzzzzzZZZOOT! zzzzZZZOOT! zZZZOOT!*"

Sagging against the door, head bowed in exhaustion, I became aware of a gentle heat. I glanced up. At the end of the landing, the assorted *yontan* glowed and flickered in the dark like giant prayer candles. I meditated on them awhile.

Then, I turned around, took a deep breath, held it, and hid behind the furnace room door as I yanked it open. Black smoke roiled out and up into the night sky.

When the furnace room cleared, I filled the shafts with new *yontan*.

I knelt before the furnace and adjusted the vents to Mrs. Han's "just a hair."

After cleansing myself of soot, I set the alarm for 4 a.m.

C. Lill Ahrens is a creative writing instructor, editorial consultant, writer's coach, published cartoonist and an editor for Calyx: A Journal of Art and Writing by Women. Her award-winning true stories are published in numerous literary journals and anthologies. She lives with her husband, Paul, in Corvallis, Oregon.

THE PARISIAN ANGEL
Paris, France

My friend Lisa is planning a trip to Paris. We are sitting in my kitchen, where she has spread out several maps and dumped a towering stack of French guidebooks on the table. Using her forefinger with its perfectly polished red nail, she points out all the places that she and her husband will visit, commenting on each exotic destination.

"Can you imagine?" she asks. "All that great food, the quaint cafés, walking along the river banks. ..." Her voice drops off as she envisions herself in such locations. Lisa, it's obvious, has already fallen under the city's spell and can't wait to return.

"Don't you just love Paris," she asks dreamily.

Frankly, I don't know how to answer. For others, Paris is the most romantic of all locales. For me, it's the city of unfinished business, where a story that was once started hasn't yet found its end.

It stems from my first impression of Paris. Lasting memories are formed by virgin encounters with the places we see, the food we eat, the bed we sleep in, and most of all, the people we meet.

I was studying in Vienna, and as any college student abroad will tell you, exploring the continent during school breaks is half the fun. There is no other feeling like grabbing your rail ticket and backpack, opening a new, crisp map of Europe on a bright and shiny Saturday morning, and picking, either on a whim or some rumor you have heard, the place that you want to visit next.

That's how I ended up on the overnight train to Paris.

I slept most of the way and awoke as I felt the wheels slow for our arrival in the French capital. Drowsily, I grabbed my backpack and searched for my small shoulder bag, the one with money and a credit card inside. It was nowhere to be found.

My shoulders slumped as I realized that I had been robbed. I couldn't figure out how. Several others and I shared the closed train compartment. I didn't remember anyone else coming in.

I left the train and decided to go to the police — if I could only find them. Stopping here and there, I asked vendors for directions. Most stared at me dumbly, amused at my English words. Finally, a woman pointed out a small police office.

A policeman in a stiff uniform and proper hat motioned for me to sit down in front of him. He sat down at his computer, and began firing away questions in French. I couldn't understand a word he said. I told him so in English, but he asked another question — in French. I just stared at him dumbly. Finally, he shrugged his shoulders and rolled his eyes with exasperation.

"*Sprechen Sie Deutsch?*" I asked. No response.

"*Hablas Español?*" I asked again. No response again.

Tired and fed up, I blurted out my story in English, pausing briefly between sentences for breath. When I stopped, the policeman stared at me a minute and then began typing in a two-fingered fashion. He did understand what I was saying! Or else he was typing, "This stupid American girl doesn't speak even one word of French. Who knows what she is gesturing wildly about?"

When he was done, the policeman spoke again in French and pointed me to the door. So that was the end of that.

Later I heard that there had been a rash of train robberies that month. Now, I was in Paris with less than 30 euros in my pocket and no credit card. A fine state!

One bright spot — before setting out for Paris, my uncle had given me the name of a place to stay. "The Palais de la Femme," he suggested. "They were very nice. And don't worry. It's cheap."

I looked at the slip of paper now, fingering the little money I had in my pockets. I hoped the hostel was really cheap; otherwise, I'd be sleeping on the street. For now, I had the whole day ahead of me, so I tossed my backpack over my shoulder and set off to at least see SOME of Paris. I grabbed a map of the subway system and went exploring.

The cozy cafés that I passed looked warm and inviting — young couples were staring at each other over tumblers of red wine. I saw children eating cakes and bread while their mothers talked happily together. I had no money to enjoy these tempting places, so I just walked on, watching these happy scenes through the windows.

Determined not to let that get to me, I hauled my backpack across the city to see the outside of Notre Dame, free to view, and I walked along the Seine River, also free.

It was getting dark as I walked into the park under the Eiffel Tower. As a recently robbed student, I couldn't afford the ticket to the top of the tower. So, I sat down on a park bench and stared at its twinkling lights. It was strange to look at a monument that I had seen so many times in pictures.

Couples walked by arm in arm, others sat on a nearby bench kissing. I was overcome with a feeling of loneliness. Suddenly, all I wanted to do was leave this City of Light and these people I couldn't understand far behind. But first, I had to find somewhere to spend the night.

I walked over to stand in the light of a pub, and pulled out my map. While I searched for the street I needed, a group of three young men noticed me. They were sitting around a tiny table, drinking wine and smoking. Their pointing fingers and rapid French made me wonder, but when they stood and wobbled toward me, I felt uneasy.

Quickly, I stuffed the map back into my pack, pulled the pack over my shoulders and walked away. One of the drunks began to follow me, speaking and joking in French. I ignored him because I had no idea what he was telling me.

A block later, I turned to see him still coming behind me. The glass of wine was gone; an intent look now covered his face.

It's nothing! I told myself. I crossed the street, noticing with sinking dread that the sun was now gone. The drunk was still following.

I was really scared. There were fewer people on the street, and the area was looking more suburban. Who could help me when I can't even speak French?

Then I saw it — Palais de la Femme — in bright lights ahead. I felt like jumping for joy. It was a nondescript building, but right then it looked like the Hilton. With one more quick glance at the man, I slipped in the door.

The place was simple and clean. At the front desk, two women were working. One, who was a young woman about my age, smiled at me.

I hesitated and took a deep breath before asking in English for a room. She smiled, but it seemed that she didn't understand very well. "*Hablas Español?*" I asked tentatively.

"*Si!*" she replied. Relieved, I asked for a room. She took out a key and then told me the price. It was about 20 euros more than I had with me. My shoulders fell and I turned to leave, stuffing my money back into my pack.

"Wait," she called, motioning me back. Then she pulled out her purse from a drawer, opened a tiny pouch and drew out several notes.

"Here, now you have enough," she said, handing me a form and pen to register.

I looked at her with shock. Did she just GIVE me money? With her simple gesture, this young woman, who told me her name was Pacquita, had turned around an entire city for me.

I thanked her profusely while she gave me the keys to the room. I have never been so relieved at the sight of clean, white sheets in a small, ugly room. For the first time that night, I took a deep breath and felt safe.

Later that evening, I went down to talk with her. She was a university student who had a French father and a Spanish mother. We talked of America and Spain and France. She told me of her studies, and I talked of my school life in Vienna.

Pacquita wasn't working that next morning, and I never saw her again. But when I left for the train station, I noticed that Paris had taken on a fresh hue. Sparkling sunlight reflected in the windows as the sleeping city woke up. I could smell baking bread and rich coffee from the cafés as I walked back to the station.

A few weeks later, back in Vienna, I got a postcard from Pacquita. "I hope you had a nice trip home, and a great year at university," she wrote in Spanish. I pinned her card up on my bulletin board, and later packed it home to America.

"That card is probably still in a box in my basement somewhere," I now tell my friend Lisa, who has been listening to my story. "I haven't thought about Pacquita for a long time.

Is it possible? Have I let the fright I felt in Paris overcome my memory of the kindness I found there? I breathe slowly, remembering how that one small gesture of compassion changed everything.

"Let me see those brochures," I say, grabbing a stack of them. I open up a map of France to see the page dotted with tiny villages, blue lakes, and then Paris, big and shiny on the page.

Maybe places, like people, deserve second chances.

"Paris really *did* look beautiful in the moonlight," I tell Lisa, a smile on my face. This French city, I have decided, is worth seeing with fresh eyes.

Janna Graber is a travel writer, editor and producer. Her writing has appeared in publications including Chicago Tribune, The Denver Post, Reader's Digest, Parade, Redbook and Alaska Airlines. She is the manag-

ing editor at Go World Travel Magazine (GoWorldTravel.com), an international publication covering the world's most fascinating people and places. Follow her at @AColoradoGirl

BEST FOOT FORWARD
Malawi

It's hard to hang on to your shoes in Africa.

Mine are being assessed by Blessings and his pal Earnest in a dusty village at the southern end of Lake Malawi. Blessings is barefoot. Earnest is padding around in a torn and flapping pair of Chinese imitation Reeboks.

The two teenagers are working the fence along the northern end of Club Makakola, a lakeside resort. They're peddling carved wooden key rings through the wire to any guests who, like me, might wander away from thatched shade and groomed sands to explore the fringes of Club Mak's fenced territory.

One flicker of interest in these rudimentary curios and I'm hooked. After some small talk through the wire I'm offered a village tour, which frankly sounds more intriguing than lounging beside the water under sun umbrellas, known locally as "gin-and-tonic trees."

I leave the confines of Club Mak, join the lads on their side of the fence and we set off through the dry bush toward their home. Both boys are stealing frequent glances at my cross-trainers.

First we meet the kindergarten kids. They've seen us coming and are clapping their hands in unison and giggling. Some are chanting "*mzungu, mzungu*" (white man, white man). For a tickle of a moment I am David Livingstone.

Blessings and Earnest lead me through a motley collection of mud huts to the village market, a collection of makeshift stalls huddled within the expansive shade thrown by an enormous mahogany tree.

Mounds of stringy, silver whitebait-like fish called kapenta are drying in the sun. Tomatoes are piled like miniature cannonballs into bright red pyramids beside juicy mangoes and stubby green bananas. Unshelled peanuts lie in loose piles on plastic sheeting. Grass baskets are filled with speckled beans.

These goods look fine, but there's little commerce. A few men sit around smoking and making more roll-ups, wrapping strips torn from the local newspaper around scrapings they've scavenged off the floor of a tobacco barn.

On one side of the market I see the shutters up at Allah the Great Shop. But Mrs. Chiwotcha's hole-in-the-wall is selling belts, bags, fly spray, knives, sodas, cough mixtures and a range of painkillers. Boxes of Panado and Cafemol are center stage, like two Shakespearean characters. They are drugs of choice in this tiny African country.

"We get too, too many headaches from the heat," explains Blessings as he instinctively rubs his temples. By midmorning it's a stifling 34 Celsius (93 Fahrenheit). I swallow another bottle of Quench bottled water and muse on the side effects of long-term Panado addiction.

We walk past more huts to another cool spot beneath a massive mango tree planted in the center of the village, under which the chief is holding court. Earnest indicates we should not intrude, adding a solemn shake of the head in emphasis.

The chief sits rotund and motionless, his white shirt tucked into a red, calf-length *kikoyu* wrapped around his waist. About 30 women sit under the tree listening to a scrawny man in shirtsleeves and creased suit pants deliver an impassioned lecture. He gestures often, emphatically, at a diagram scrawled on a large sheet of cardboard.

Blessings explains that the slim speaker is a health department official giving advice to mothers with young babies. We listen to his harangue. His audience remains impassive despite his animated delivery.

Blessings and Earnest are eager to move on and steer me elsewhere. Their eyes watch my every step, glued to my shoes. There isn't much else to see, just more huts and a couple of shacks built from corrugated iron scraps. An emaciated dog slinks out from sight. It's not what you see in the Africa brochures.

My ad hoc excursion ends at a dusty hut, which turns out to be the village gift shop. Stepping into its dark interior I see a modest stash of wooden salad bowls, carved utensils, domino sets and chessboards — any of which I can have, says Earnest, in exchange for my shoes.

I tell him that, sadly, I really do need my shoes. Instead I offer to buy some dominos perhaps or maybe a small bowl. "Is that OK?"

"It's OK," they both reply dismissively, shrugging their shoulders in unison. Earnest is now flicking glances that bounce off my shoelaces.

I pick up a small black wooden bowl. "So how much?"

"Ah, this eez the real ebony," says Blessings immediately.

"Is there any other?"

Blessings studies me a moment, then cracks a huge smile; a flash of bright white enamel that pierces the surrounding gloom.

"There eez the ebony nam - bah - wan," he advises solemnly, dragging out the words and widening his eyes, then adds almost as an afterthought, "and there eez the ebony nam-bah-two."

I know ebony is rare and a protected wood in Malawi. I guess the bowl in question is either Blackwood or some other hardwood. "And so this bowl then, how much?"

Without a moment's hesitation Blessings fires back: "That one? Well that one, she's a very, very, nam-bah-wan wan!"

I laugh at this excellent indigenous riposte. Blessings is on a roll.

"This one she's a very, very good one," he persists. "You like it too much, no?"

What can I say? I like it too very much I say. Blessings grins. Earnest grins. We do the deal. I hand over some kwacha notes and put the bowl in my day bag. I then tell them that, no, I don't also need a wooden key ring with a name carved on it. "It's not bad," I say, "but no thanks."

"But very cheap," offers Earnest, his eyes twitching, still fixated on my sneakers.

"Sorry," I repeat, "but that's no good for me. You see my name is Rob and that key ring says Sue. So go find a Sue."

Spray bursts from Blessings' lips as he snorts with mirth. "HA HA HA, no, no, no," he splutters, vigorously shaking his head. Earnest at last stops staring at my shoes to look me straight in the eye, which is quite un-nerving.

Earnest speaks. "Hey, you pretty funny sort of guy. Where you from? Where's your country?" Before I can answer, he adds, "we carve your name, we put your name there!" His stubby finger stabs at the wooden disc.

I'm defeated. The boys have won again. My key ring order is agreed, my name written on a scrap of brown paper, after which we stroll back to the beach. Earnest is living up to his name, ever ready with raised eyebrow, pointing at his chest, nodding his head, eyes dancing over my shoes.

I explain once again that I really do need my shoes and that I can't simply take them off and hand them over. I tell them I have no other shoes and point out that while Earnest at least has something on his feet, poor Blessings is barefoot. I appeal to their sense of fair play. "I can't give a pair of shoes to one and not the other." Besides, I add, my shoes are too small. They won't fit their broad feet. No way!

On hearing this the two boys stop in their tracks, look down at their own feet and then again at my shoes. The truth is evident. They assume expressions that are heart-wrenchingly downcast. I consider handing over some cash in lieu of shoes but decide against it.

My heart is heavy. We've reached an impasse at the gates of Club Mak. But I can't simply say goodbye and walk away. So I promise Blessings and Earnest that I will send them something once I get home. An instant dulling of their eyes suggests they've heard this one before. But they scribble their names and village address in my notebook anyway.

What Blessings and Earnest truly desire are brand-name shoes like mine, not the cheap Chinese fakes they see available in local shops. Even though they can't afford even those imports they do know the difference even if owning a pair of genuine Reeboks is beyond their wildest dreams.

Early next morning we meet at the agreed time beside the resort fence and the boys hand over two carved key rings. We say farewell and they depart, their eyes still lingering on the pair of shoes that got away.

A few days later I'm farther south at Ku Chawe Inn, a small hotel tucked into forested slopes on the Zomba Plateau south of the lake. Far below, hidden by cloud, is the town of Zomba.

Mist hugs the land, obscuring any views beyond a co- lossal mango tree, rows of red canna and the clipped green lawns in the inn's gardens.

The previous evening I'd sat at the hotel bar still thinking about Blessings and Earnest and their yearning for a pair of decent shoes.

Once home I make good my promise, bundling some T-shirts and shorts around two pairs of running shoes. The air postage to Malawi is horrendous but sea mail will take maybe months, with even less guarantee of the package arriving safely. I post my gift care of Club Makakola and include a cover letter of explanation with the names of the two teenagers and their village.

Do Blessings and Earnest ever get their shoes? I don't know, but I like to think my parcel did eventually make it. If any of you reading this should ever visit Club Makakola on Lake Malawi, please take a short stroll to the resort fence to see if there are two young hawkers wearing genuine Reebok trainers.

Rob Woodburn is a freelance travel writer and blogger based in Sydney, Australia.

UNFINISHED CHAPTERS
Hawaii, USA

"Hey! Want your picture taken with Tom Selleck?"

I immediately looked around to see who had asked. Well, who could blame me? I clearly fit the criteria of the question's targeted demographic: (1) I was female, (2) I was breathing and (3) I was a fan of *Magnum, P.I.*

It was the second day of my stay on the island of Oahu in Hawaii and, like every good tourist, I was aggressively doing my bit for the economy by trolling the aisles of the Waikiki Shopping Plaza on Kalakaua Avenue in Honolulu. It was a six-story mall offering everything from sunglasses, flip-flops and chocolate macadamia nuts to upscale fashions, Asian antiques and high-end restaurants.

Tucked into the corner of the first floor with a tripod, Polaroid camera and a cardboard cut-out of Selleck was a goofy-grinned, shaggy-haired young guy about my age who, in retrospect, could have been an Irish cousin of Owen Wilson if the latter had embraced reddish-gold highlights.

"Step right up, pretty lady. One for $5 or three for 15! What'll it be?"

I pointed out the absence of any savings on a multiple purchase.

He snapped his fingers in preface to an even snappier reply. "You know, you're the only person who's ever caught that? I should give you a discount just for being smart."

Equally quick with a quip, I asked if he was aware that his charismatic prop wasn't the real deal.

Not missing a beat, he did a double-take, smacked himself in the forehead and proclaimed, "Oh man! The dude I bought this from totally ripped me off!" With arms akimbo, he stood there as if contemplating what to do next.

"I suppose he could look real from the right distance," I suggested.

"Like where? Maybe Connecticut?"

Call it silly, but I've always viewed a sense of humor as a major plus, not to mention that he was pretty obviously flirting with me. Besides, anyone that unabashed about hawking a cheesy gimmick could probably use all the sales he could get. "Five dollars it is then," I declared.

As I started to open my purse, he insisted I didn't have to pay until I saw the picture. "It could be completely awful," he warned.

"I'm sure that's a given," I agreed, "but it doesn't affect the fun."

Half an hour and two dozen poses later — he kept insisting Tom had blinked — we were still talking. His name was Nick and he had moved to Waikiki from Los Angeles three years previous to hone his photography skills. Naturally, I couldn't resist teasing him about his progress.

"Oh, I just do this stuff for fun," he explained, "and to use Tom as a chick-magnet."

"How's that working for you?"

He winked. "You tell me."

"You must have a very understanding wife."

"Nope. Not even a girlfriend." He leaned forward to add in whispered postscript that he wasn't gay, either.

I reminded him that the chick-magnet line had already canceled that possibility.

"Then I guess that just leaves international jewel thief and ax-wielding psychopath." He mugged his best impressions of both.

"Well, since I'm not wearing jewelry and I don't see an ax, my guess is that it would be safe to ask if you're doing anything for dinner?" Even as the words came out of my mouth, I couldn't quite believe I was saying them. I was, after all, a product of the generation that believed girls never telephoned boys, much less asked them out.

Yet a Tarot reading I'd had only that morning hinted I was on the cusp of discovering bold and exciting adventures if I did something completely spontaneous and out of character.

"I just happen to get off at 6," he replied, flattered by the invitation. "But I'd never hear the end of it from my parents if I told 'em I'd let you buy."

*****

It wasn't until we entered the crowded beach-side eatery that he casually asked if I minded cooking my own dinner.

"Excuse me?"

"Steak, chicken, ribs — it all comes with its own instructions," he continued, "so there's not much chance of burning the place down…"

Shortly after he came to Waikiki, he explained, he'd made friends with a couple of guys who had just launched their new restaurant and bar, the Shore Bird. Practically overnight, the concept of marrying an all-you-can-eat salad bar to a DIY barbecue was a hit with everyone who came through its doors. He laughed when I remarked that most people go on vacation to get *out* of a kitchen. "You never know who you could rub elbows with at the grill," he said.

"Even Tom Selleck?"

"Nah. He's kinda freaky around flames," Nick said. "Being cardboard 'n' all…"

Over a meal that began with mai tais and ended with shared scoops of macadamia nut ice cream, we traded stories about ourselves. Mine was that of a writer and touring theater director who paid the bills with a full-time job as a legal secretary. Nick's parents ran a bookkeeping company in San Diego and were disappointed that numbers just hadn't been his calling.

He asked what sort of sights I'd seen since my arrival. As I proceeded to tell him, he nodded in amusement and remarked, "Ah, Waikiki 101. All the tourist stuff." Since his schedule was pretty much his own, he offered to be my personal tour guide. "We can start tomorrow," he said. "Where shall I pick you up?"

Having done enough solo traveling, I knew it was unwise to give out hotel information to a stranger. At the same time, I obviously felt trusting enough to let this same stranger drive. "You can meet me out front at the Royal Hawaiian," I told him.

He grinned and complimented me on my choice of accommodations, not knowing that I was staying at a much smaller and more economical address three streets away. In those early days of free-spirited adventure, I loved walking through the lobbies of elegant hotels with my morning cup of coffee, saying hello to people, and pretending I was a guest. I don't know whether it ever occurred to me that this might be frowned on by the management since all I was doing was passing through. For all I knew, maybe that's what everyone else was doing and *no one* was really staying there.

"Just for the record," Nick suddenly volunteered, "I'm not looking for anything beyond friendship right now." He and his last girlfriend had recently broken up, he explained, and it would be a long time before he completely sorted out how he felt about it. Coming from anyone else, it might have sounded exactly like a line to invite pursuit rather than dissuade it, but I took it at face value, especially since I wasn't looking for a new romance, either.

As we were leaving the restaurant, a buddy at the bar waved him over to say hello. "Any news on Lia?" I heard the friend ask him. "Couple more weeks," Nick replied, forcing a smile. The friend asked him to call if he heard anything.

"I couldn't help but overhear," I confessed. "Is everything OK?"

"I don't know," he cryptically replied. "I honestly don't." Though his response forbade further inquiry, it nevertheless had riddled my curiosity.

He insisted on walking me back to my supposed hotel and gave me a light kiss on the cheek. "Can you be ready at 6:30?" he asked.

"I thought we were doing something during daylight."

"We are. I meant 6:30 in the morning. You OK with that?"

Though I couldn't for the life of me imagine where we were going, I confessed to being a morning person. "Anything else I need to know?"

"Sunscreen and walking shoes," he instructed. "Oh, and maybe some insect repellent."

What had I gotten myself into?

*****

I remembered he had taken his coffee black the previous night and I decided not to show up empty-handed the next morning. Like clockwork he was waiting in a funky Jeep that had seen better days and probably even fewer car washes.

He eyed the purse I'd brought along. "You don't have any pork in there, do you?"

"Why would I have pork?'

"Given our destination, it would be very bad luck." The reason Oahu had a wet (windward) side and a dry (leeward) side, he said, was because of an ancient lovers' spat between the fire goddess Pele and her boyfriend Kamapua'a, who was half man/half pig. "If you bring anything to her side of the island that reminds her of him, there's no telling what she'll do."

"She sounds dangerous."

"Only when she's mad. The rest of the time she wanders around the Hilton Hawaiian Village in a scarlet muumuu and vanishes if anyone talks to her."

"So where are we going that requires such an early start?" I asked.

"Best view on the island. Uh — you're not afraid of heights, are you?"

"No, I'm good."

"How 'bout rickety stairs and dark tunnels?"

"Come again?"

He laughed. "We're going to scale the Brow of the Tuna."

In all my perusing of tourist guides, this was a new one to me.

"Actually it was only the first Hawaiians that ever called it that," he explained. "To everyone else, it's just Diamond Head."

In postcards, brochures and travel programs, it's one of Hawaii's most iconic landmarks, an extinct volcano rising 760 feet to a breathtaking panoramic lookout. Remnants of stone bunkers and cannon emplacements can still be found on the crater, testament to Honolulu's early military defense system against sea- and ground-based attacks.

Nineteenth-century sailors, Nick explained during our climb, had been mesmerized by tricks of the light to think that the crater was peppered with diamonds that would make them rich. Instead, the shimmer they saw was nothing more than shiny calcite crystals. In other words, worthless.

"I can see why you wanted to come early," I said. We weren't even halfway to the top and another toasty day was already beginning. A veteran hiker, Nick had packed two plastic bottles of water, a flashlight for the tunnels, and some granola bars to munch on during our breaks for pictures.

"Of course there's only one bad thing about making it all the way to the top," he said.

"What's that?"

"Having to go back down the same way." At least beating the crowds, he added, meant we wouldn't be sharing narrow trails with people on their way up.

When we reached the highest point of the crater, "feeling on top of the world" became more than just an expression of euphoria. I was actually quite proud of myself for accomplishing something so radically outside my city-girl comfort zone.

Nick was shading his eyes and looking out to sea when I thanked him for showing me this priceless view.

The glisten of a trickled teardrop on his cheekbone didn't escape my notice.

"Allergies," he said, and put his sunglasses back on.

*****

"You're not afraid of ghosts, are you?" he asked en route to the next site he wanted to show me.

"This is becoming a pattern," I remarked as I let myself in the passenger side.

"What?"

"You're asking me these things when it's too late to back out."

He assured me that the ghosts in question weren't scary, just mournful. "They've had almost 200 years to wonder if they made the right choice…"

We were making a different type of ascent now, this one 200+ feet higher via Route 61. Unlike the dry, desolate crater we had just left behind, the cliffs of the Koolau Mountain Range were lush with vibrant vegetation. It was also incredibly windy, enough to almost blow me off my feet when we reached the top. The signage at the lookout point advising parents to hold tightly to their children's hands affirmed just how gusty it could get.

As if to punctuate the warning, we watched two college-age guys futilely chase their wind-snatched baseball caps to the railing. Their howls of laughter at the loss of their headwear, however, were tame by comparison to what sounded like a chilling chorus of banshees as we drew nearer to the edge.

The bloodiest battle of Kamehameha's quest to unite the islands, Nick explained, had ended here at Nuuanu Pali. Trapped between the invading army and a sheer cliff that dropped 1,000 feet below, the defeated warriors had no choice but to jump to their deaths or be pushed.

"That doesn't sound like much of a choice," I said.

Nick said that it depended on whether you wanted to own your decision or let someone else make it for you.

I couldn't help but feel that it wasn't just Hawaiian history we were talking about.

*****

I knew what shave ice was. I had just never had any. Nick was astonished, and announced that it was only fitting my first experience be with the best shave ice shack on the island. The frozen treat, he explained, was originally introduced by Japanese immigrants who worked in the sugar cane fields. "By the time they started moving off the plantations to open their own grocery stores, shave ice was their biggest seller." His friends Tookie and Rita, he said, favored a simple country life but certainly didn't mind that their humble enterprise was on the University of Hawaii's flagship campus. "When you're older than dirt," he added, "you like seeing young people."

We were wending our way through the Manoa Valley — a richly vegetated landscape that reminded me a lot of Northern California. The sublime sense of quiet made it hard to believe we weren't that far from the bustle of Waikiki. It was raining intermittently at this point, a daily occurrence that went a long way in not only explaining why everything was so green but also why there were so many mini-waterfalls, rivulets and rainbows.

"If you're up for another hike," he offered, "I can show you a bamboo forest and the base of the Koolaus Mountains."

I had to confess that Diamond Head alone had left me hiked-out for one day.

"No prob." The rain, he noted, was looking to preempt a trek up to Manoa Falls, anyway. Accumulated water on the concrete stepping stones and wood bridges throughout the trail could make their surfaces dangerously slick for someone inexperienced; i.e., me. "And then there's the mosquitoes," he said. "I'm guessing you wouldn't be keen about them, either…"

We had reached our destination. Yes, "shack" was an apt description. In fact, a second shack had been bolted onto the first and this, Nick told me, was where Tookie and Rita lived. As if on cue, the wizened pair emerged, reminding me of rustic dolls whose heads were made from dried apples and whose eyes were black cloves. Between the two of them, I doubted they had more than six teeth, and yet there was no mistaking the unabashed joy with which they both rushed to greet Nick. He introduced me as his California friend, and Rita set at once to making us the treat we had come for.

As she did so, Nick related that Tookie had known from the first moment he saw Rita that they would marry and live happily ever after.

"High school sweethearts?" I asked.

Nick shook his head. "Sandbox playmates." Tookie's father had been a fisherman; Rita's mother had worked as a hotel maid. Since neither could take their children to work with them, they enlisted a friend who had several children of her own. "From that first day of play, they were inseparable." They soon would celebrate their 68th anniversary. "That's really the way to do it," Nick continued. "Meet the love of your life in a sandbox and never spend a single moment apart."

As Rita handed Nick his cup of shave ice, she pulled him down as if to whisper in his ear.

"No," he replied with a smile. "She's just visiting for the week."

*****

Dinner that night was a family-friendly Italian restaurant in the Royal Hawaiian Shopping Center. "I know it's only a short walk next door to your hotel," he said, "but how 'bout a stroll on the beach?"

Given the heaviness of the meal we'd just finished, it sounded like the perfect way to walk it off.

Just past the beachside Waikiki police station, I noticed a cluster of four large boulders. "Waikiki has its own Stonehenge?" I quipped.

Nick put on his "mysterious" face and his voice dropped to a whisper. "That's not as far off as you think." Nicknamed the Wizard Stones, they were believed to have curative powers placed within by four healers who came to the island around 400 A.D. "Nobody knew where these guys came from but when it was time for them to return home, they promised the islanders that they'd endow the rocks with the magical 'mana' to fix whatever ailed them."

Ancient legends, he said, still exerted a tight grip on native Hawaiians even in the 20th century. "The locals — especially elders — know better than to ever walk past the Wizard Stones without bowing their heads in respect or leaving a fresh flower."

I asked him how he knew so much of the island's history.

"I had a good teacher," he replied.

Whether it was the red wine we had at dinner that loosened his tongue, the moonlight on the Pacific that conjured bittersweet memories, or maybe just the need to unburden his aching heart to a total stranger, he began to tell me who that teacher was.

*****

Nick didn't really know anyone when he first came to the islands. A month later, he felt like he had lived there all his life. He found a roommate, got a job, bought the Jeep. Life was good. It was suddenly made even better the day he met Lia.

"It wasn't the stuff of movies," he reminisced. "It was at an ABC store." She had gone in to buy some scented hand lotion for her grandmother; he was there to buy some beef jerky. They reached the cash register at the same time from opposite sides. "From the moment she first smiled," he paused. "You can see why I relate to Tookie and Rita. I just knew. And so did she."

There were obstacles to romance, however. Lia was a fourth-generation Hawaiian whose family took pride in ancestral connections to royalty. He was a red-headed haole from middle-class parents on the mainland. "We kept our dating a secret for a long time, even though we were spending all of our free time together. She told her parents she was out with friends. They just didn't know it was only one friend and that it was yours truly." It was Lia who had introduced him to all of the places and all of the stories he'd been sharing with me.

"Because she had never lived anywhere else, she couldn't imagine ever leaving. And so even though Hawaii was only supposed to be a year or two gig for me, I started rethinking what it would be like to stay if we got married." None of that could happen, of course, unless her parents gave their consent.

The ugliness that ensued was more than either could have imagined. "We decided to just chill for a little while until they calmed down. We were sending messages through friends and sneaking off whenever we could, but it's not something we knew we could keep up."

The hammer fell with a resounding crash when she told him her parents were marrying her off. "She didn't love the guy. She barely even knew him but enough to know that he drank, flirted with anything in a skirt, and had more than a passing interest in her parents' bank account."

Nick and Lia were together for the last time about two weeks before the wedding. "Neither of us could stop crying because we knew nothing we could do could change the future." He had contemplated packing up and just going home at that point, but couldn't bring himself to do it.

"A few months ago, she called to tell me she was pregnant and was going to have a little girl."

"Is the —"

He interrupted the question before I had even finished. "I pray every night that the baby's his," he said, "because I can't imagine what will happen if it looks like me."

We had walked all the way to the beach across from Kapiolani Park and he motioned me to a bench where we could rest before heading back. "Best view there is," he proclaimed, pointing overhead to a velvet black sky which looked as if someone tossed a handful of diamonds against it and they had all stuck. I wondered how many of the stars he had wished upon, or how many times he sat on this very spot with Lia.

"Promise me," he said, "that you'll never sit on this bench again unless it's with someone special."

"Only if you promise the same," I replied, curious as to what had brought this about. The only thing clear was that he had said as much about Lia as his broken heart allowed him to.

*****

For the remainder of my vacation, Nick was intent on giving me as many non-city adventures as he could think of, cementing memories to last a lifetime.

I can't, for instance, drink Kona coffee without remembering the coffee farm and cocoa orchards overlooking the island's North Shore. Despite my encasing three pounds of coffee bean purchases in resealable plastic bags, the inside of my suitcase held their aroma for at least eight months after.

I remember the dank smell of Kaneana Cave, touted in Hawaiian legend as the birthplace of mankind. As we explored its spooky interior, Nick regaled me with stories of the shape-shifting Nanaue, who would charm victims as a handsome young man, invite them to join him for an ocean swim, then revert to his true form as a bloodthirsty shark. "Never go swimming in the Pacific with a strange man," he warned me. "You just never know…"

In Honolulu, we took a walk around Aliiōlani Hale, the Supreme Court building, and came upon the largest banyan tree I'd ever seen. According to Nick, an orphanage had occupied this area in the early-19th century, and the tangled network of ghoulish gray roots that dropped from the tree's thick branches were said to walk at night in search of the souls of lost children.

We rode horses in the Kaaawa Valley. I not only came away with the sore muscles to prove it, but I'm also pretty sure that the wicked cold I caught after my return home was from the downpour we were caught in with our fellow riders.

On my last full day, we took a drive to the leeward side of the island. I kept pointing out beautifully pristine

— and curiously empty — beaches that I thought would be a good spot for our picnic lunch. Nick set me straight that this less-crowded side of Oahu had made it a magnet for homeless people trying to live off the grid and drug dealers looking to score without witnesses. To this day, I remember what he said whenever I see an idyllic spot that's just a little too perfect.

The next morning, he insisted on taking me to the airport. "What time shall I swing by your hotel?"

"I should probably make a confession," I said. "I'm not really staying at the Royal Hawaiian."

He winked. "I knew that." The first evening, he explained, he had run into someone he knew, stopped to chat and just happened to notice my leaving. "My mom always raised me to make sure my date got home safely. I've been looking out for you the whole time."

*****

This being the era before intensified Transportation Security Administration precautions, Nick walked me to my gate. As boarding was called, he gave me a brotherly hug and a kiss on the forehead. "*A hui hou*," he said. "Until we meet again."

The irony is that neither one of us spoke about exchanging addresses and phone numbers and staying in touch. I was reminded of how many other touch-and-go moments each of us have throughout the course of our lives. The casual conversations we have in line at the grocery store. The seat companions with whom we're thrown together on an airline flight. The kindred spirits we spend a few days with at a writers' conference. They reel us in with the start of a story — as do we — leaving us to speculate "so what happened next?" long after we part company.

Now and again — and with greater frequency as I get older — I've taken the step of saying, "Let's continue this conversation, shall we?" The technology of e-mail and the expediency of social media has obviously made it easier to keep these promises. Yet even if they had existed on the day we said farewell, I don't know that I would have done anything different than to hug him back and tell him I hoped everything worked out.

*****

It was almost four years before I got back to Waikiki. I went by the shopping mall but he and Tom Selleck were no longer there. I was going to look him up in the phone book but realized that the passage of time had caused me to forget his last name.

I found myself revisiting some of the places we had gone, though not with the same level of daring as when I'd had an intrepid companion who knew the island like the back of his hand. I walked by the Wizard Stones and left an orchid lei. I cooked my own dinner at the Shore Bird and took a seat facing the entrance in the event he walked in. I took countless pictures of Diamond Head, still marveling that I had actually hiked to the top.

And on my last full day, I took a walk in the direction of the beach at Kapiolani Park. Although I hadn't brought anyone special with me, I felt a tug to see if I could find the exact bench in the middle of the day that we had shared on a star-bright evening.

What I never expected to see among the day's sun-worshippers was a father and his red-headed little girl running around and around that very bench with whoops of glee. The moment he scooped her up in his arms and pointed to the brightly colored catamarans out on the water — a gesture she eagerly imitated — I knew exactly who I was looking at.

A part of me wanted to draw closer, to go up and re-introduce myself. The part that prevailed, however, was the one that continued to watch thoughtfully from the distance, smile to myself, and then start the long walk back to my hotel.

For all of the unfinished chapters we encounter — and all the questions they conjure which tease and linger — the only thing I needed to know about this one is that, from where I stood, it looked like it was destined for a happily ever after.

Christina Hamlett is a media relations expert and award-winning author whose credits include 30 books, 156 stage plays, five optioned feature films, and hun-

dreds of articles and interviews that appear online and in national/international trade publications. In addition, she is a script consultant for the film industry (which means she stops lots of really bad movies from coming to theaters near you) and a professional ghostwriter (which does not mean she talks to dead people). Learn more about her at authorhamlett.com.

A WITNESS TO COURAGE
United Arab Emirates

Amit made a few phone calls to arrange the transportation. There was no bus to the Abu Dhabi airport, so I would have to take a taxi.

"Be sure to only give him 40 dirhams, no more," he cautioned as I waited with my bag. Soon, a worn-out white Toyota Camry pulled up, with no taxi markings at all.

The driver was a young South Asian man, maybe in his early 30s, with thick, short, dark hair, a mustache, and large, beady eyes. He immediately stepped out of the car to help put my bag in the trunk.

The back seat was dirty. With a smile, the driver motioned me to sit in front.

I looked back at Amit.

"Thank you so much for your hospitality. You were a fantastic host," I said, trying to express my gratitude with weak words.

"Take care, and happy journeys," he replied. We shook hands.

"Keep in touch," I said, getting into the car and shutting the door. Amit watched from the parking lot until we drove out of sight, the same way Mom and Dad had stood at the train doors, watching Ashvin and I for as long as they could.

We started out the drive quietly, the man — like every taxi driver I'd met in the Emirates —adhering to the master-servant dynamic. Don't speak unless spoken to, unless the passenger is one of your people. I am also South Asian, but he could tell I wasn't like him.

I was determined to break this dynamic. At home, I rarely spoke to the talkative taxi drivers. But what I'd seen the past few days had made me curious. Here was my chance to get to know a true migrant worker.

"So…" I started, speaking slowly, "where are you from?"

He immediately smiled. "I'm from Bangladesh. Where are you going?" he asked me.

"Nepal," I replied. He looked surprised.

"You are Nepali?" he asked.

"No, I'm from America…" There was a pause, as I debated waiting for the inevitable question. But he seemed genuinely friendly, so I decided not to force any awkwardness. "But my parents are from India."

"Oh. You speak Hindi?" he asked.

"No. Only Telugu," I said.

We zipped onto the freeway, the traffic remarkably light, the streetlights dull, either due to the vast sky or the light-sucking sand. We went out of Abu Dhabi into the interior desert of the Arabian Peninsula.

Amit, the previous evening, had explained to me how divided Emirati society is in terms of race, ethnicity and religion. At his work, there are official, separate pay scales for different races (Emiratis on top, whites second, Indians at the bottom) for doing the exact same work. Even below that were the taxi drivers. There were no politics to speak of in this dictatorship, no civil rights. What would a rich westerner or Emirati have to say to a poor taxi driver?

"How long have you been in Abu Dhabi?"

"Fif years," he said, holding his hand out. Five years.

As I asked him more about his life, he warmed up. He had previously worked in an electronics shop that had been closed down by the police, and it sounded similar to the ones I'd seen below Amit's apartment. Without any choice, he was forced to become an illegal driver. This taxi — aged, its seats faded, holes and tears on the steering wheel and console, and somewhat jerky engine — was his only source of income now, almost all of which he sent back home. What a tough life.

"Well, thank you for taking me to the airport," I told him, unable to think of a better response. He smiled and reached down below his seat and pulled up a thermos and some plastic cups. With one hand on the steering wheel, he poured some liquid into a cup and handed it to me.

"Here," he said. "Bengali chai."

I held the cup for a second, wondering if this was safe. It was warm against my hand, and I just couldn't refuse genuine friendliness, so I took a sip. The flavors of spices and steamed milk flowed down my throat. It tasted aged, but was good.

"Very good. Did you make this yourself?"

He beamed, "Yes. You can't find Bengali chai here."

I sipped the tea as he asked me about my family. I wish that I'd been more prepared, and made a mental note to keep the photos of my parents and brother in my daypack rather than in my backpack, now in the trunk. I could tell he would have loved to see them.

"What about your family?" I asked. For the first time, I caught a glimmer of emotion in his eyes.

"I have three kids, all in Bangladesh," he said.

"Oh," I said. He was here, working alone, for his family. I was touched.

He reached down again and pulled out a photo album, breaking all the rules of driving, though with the light traffic, I wasn't too worried. He opened it up, searching for the right page, with one hand on the wheel.

"When did you last go to Bangladesh?"

"Two years ago. Here," he pointed. The photo could have come from one of Amama's old family albums. An old woman wearing a blue sari was in the center, surrounded by three small children — a girl, a boy and an infant. Like my family's old photos, no one was smiling: The woman was tired and cranky; the children, scared and aloof.

"My mom," he said, "and my three children."

I moved closer to see the photo better. Behind them was a tiny shack, metal sheets over a bed, cluttered. I presumed that this was their home, barely larger than my room back in Kansas.

I had a flashback to one of our trips to India, when we went to the home of one of my great-uncles. He lived far away from the rest of the family, in a much poorer part of Hyderabad. His home, which he shared with his children and a few grandchildren, was the size of a single bedroom in America, divided into two, with two beds, a tiny kitchen, and housing five or more people, depending on the night. They were ecstatic to have us there, and eager to please, offering us food, drinks, seemingly everything in their kitchen. At the time, as a shy teenager, I remember being eager to leave. Yet the impression had stuck with me all these years.

The home in the photo was far worse than my great-uncle's home. The walls were no more than metal sheet, so even a mild gale could blow them over. It was obvious that it was a slum dwelling, a neighborhood I'd never venture into on my own. Until now, at least. I made another mental note to visit some slums in Asia, and understand the lives of people living there.

"How old are they?" I asked, pointing to the children.

"She, my daughter, is 4, my oldest son is 3." He paused for a second before continuing, "And my youngest son is 1 1/2."

As he said the last age, he paused, and I could again see the hesitation in his eyes. One-and-a-half. He'd just told me that he had not returned to Bangladesh in two years.

The truth hit me, sucking my smiles dry. He had never seen his son. I felt a knot in my stomach. His only income was from being an illegal taxi driver, probably making only a fraction of what he had made at the electronics shop, sending as much as he could to his family so they could survive. My fare would be going to the family he loved and missed dearly.

Never seeing his son. I let it sink in. I couldn't imagine how that must feel.

For a few seconds, we drove in silence. Then I asked him to show me more photos. We chatted over images of his beautiful family all the way to the airport. I was glad to be in this taxi, with this man whose loneliness was so apparent. At the airport — after he walked me to the security line, an obvious gesture of friendship, and after I'd given him the money, 40 dirhams as Amit had told me, all the cash I had — we bid a short farewell. I wished him the best.

Later, I sat in the gate area awaiting my plane, and wondered. My mom had told me how, when she was young, my grandpa worked for the railroads, often away from home for months, sending money so that his three children could attend private schools and get an education. How lonely was he, so far from his children? But without his sacrifice, I would never have been born in America, or had the chance to go on this trip. It was the same thing that my Bangladeshi taxi driver, whose name I never asked, was doing here in Abu Dhabi.

Could I ever be as brave as my taxi driver or my grandpa, or make the sacrifices they did? Shaking my head, I sighed. I knew the answer.

Nithin Coca is a freelance writer who aims to build channels of communication around common challenges. He alternates between a home in California and working on social projects in Africa and Asia. As a writer, he hopes to open minds, create understanding and spur action, even if it's small, in tackling the world's problems. His pieces have appeared in Al-Jazeera, Motherboard, Quartz, Citylab and regional publications in Southeast Asia. His first book, Traveling Softly and Quietly, is available on Amazon.com.

A MONK, A SUPERSTAR AND A LIFE-ALTERING LESSON
Bhutan

I was beat. The ascent was tougher than I'd imagined and we were only halfway up. Within the next half-hour it was going to turn dark, and though the drizzle had stopped, the dark clouds hovered. My fear about slipping on the return descent was slowly intensifying into unjustified anger. Inevitably, my husband became the target.

As I struggled to lift my leaden legs — huffing, puffing and ranting — I knew I was being unreasonable. After all, we are on a holiday in Bhutan, one of the most beautiful countries in the world. I was the one who had convinced us that I can manage the trek, a few kilometers north of capital Thimphu, a sort of mock drill for the strenuous hike to Taktsang monastery coming up in a few days.

Moreover, the place was beautiful: deep forest, rolling hills, rhododendron trees (the flowers were not blooming though), birds chirping in eager excitement to settle for the night, and just the two of us. Anger seemed so grossly misplaced. But an untrained mind, an exhausted lung and tired legs understand no logic; I began to bicker. Unexpectedly, a few yards away next to a bend in the trail, we spotted five young lamas squatting and chatting. As we approached, they looked up and smiled.

As a rule, my husband had taught me to never ask how much farther to go midway on a trek; what you hear can dip the morale. An angry woman, I turned hoydenish, deciding right then to defy him.

"How far is the monastery?" I panted to the group, halting to grab a breath. "Oh, not too far," the shortest among them said in a lilting accent. I should have seen through his fib, especially since he offered to show us an alternate track. "Come, I'm going there," he said. "It will take less time."

I wish it had taken more.

The young Bhutanese lama — he couldn't have been more than 16-17 — picked up a red cloth bag from a rock on the ground, slung it on his right shoulder and motioned for us to follow. He was a couple of inches taller than I (I am short, so he couldn't classify as tall); he was also of slight build but not skinny. Crowning his fair round face was the customary shaved head. A gazelle in crimson robes, the lama nimbly climbed up, making small talk along the way, the kind most locals make with "outsiders:" how long had we been in Bhutan, did we like it, what places we had seen.

I struggled to walk. My suspicions had proved right and the lama had made us ditch the faintly marked trail — already confirming to be tough for me — opting instead for a steeper switchback. Perhaps I was too tired, or it was just my notion that lamas should stay away from women (or the other way around), I contributed nothing to the conversation, preferring to listen to the two voices — my husband's reassuring soft inflections and the lama's indeterminate accent. Now that my husband and I were no longer alone, I had stopped carping. I was relaxed, certain now that whatever happened, we wouldn't get lost. Also, listening to the banter of the two, I had forgotten about my aching feet. It's a wonder how a minor distraction can dissipate anger and anxiety.

I was chiding myself for my churlishness when I heard a squeal. "You're from India?" the lama exclaimed, as he turned around. Instantly, his verbal and body languages changed. He stopped and, clasping his hands in a perfect *namaste*, asked, "Do you speak Hindi?"

As we nodded that it was our national language, his eyes sparkled. "*Main aapse Hindi mein baat karoonga* (I will talk to you in Hindi)," he declared in chaste Hindi with no hint of an accent. We were stunned. Though In-

dia and Bhutan share close relations — economic, politi-
cal, geographic and social — in the three days we had
been there no one had hinted at any working knowledge
of Hindi, let alone wanting to speak it.

"Your Hindi is better than mine," my husband genuinely complimented him. "Films," the lama laughed. "I
have learned Hindi watching your films."

I was shocked, for no particular reason other than the
presumption that lamas are God's children. I had always
believed that they must be isolated and protected from
the world's evil influences. Movies? Crass dialogues?
Romance? It seemed blasphemous.

We had been hiking together for almost 10 minutes,
but our quota of shock and scandal for the day had only
just begun. "*Kareena mujhe bahut achchi lagti hai* (I
like Kareena Kapoor, a Bollywood superstar, a lot)," the
lama said.

I was holding my husband's hand for balance, otherwise I think I would have slipped. The lama said how he
had liked the actress from her first film "Refugee" and
how he dreamed of her every night. This was contrary to
what I had believed "acceptable" for a man of religion.

"Saif Ali Khan won't like that," my husband teased
him. "Why?" the lama asked innocently.

"Because," my husband explained, "she is his wife."

As if trying to console himself, our new friend piped
up: "She should've married Shah Rukh (Shah Rukh
Khan, also a Bollywood star)." But he is already married, my husband informed him. "Shah Rukh bhi (he

too)?" The poor lama was clearly having a tough time soaking it all in.

So was I. I was bewildered that a lama should be allowed to watch Hindi movies and admit his "love"— no matter how innocuous — for a film star. Shouldn't he be studying his religious scriptures instead of defiling his mind with inanities like make-believe movies?

Perturbed and uncomprehending, I broke my silence and asked him point blank how he was allowed to watch films.

"*Kyon nahin* (why not)?" he countered, looking at me perhaps for the first time. Pursing his lips, and darting his eyes from my husband to me, he began explaining.

What followed was an eye-opener. The bemused lama told us that Buddhism is an outward-looking and open religion.

"We are encouraged to see the world through movies, music, the Internet and books," he said. All lamas, he informed us, read up on every conceivable topic — from Chinese transgressions in Tibet to Justin Bieber's on-off relationship with Selena Gomez, from global warming to Formula 1, from America's economic policies to noir movies; pulp fiction, international relations, rock music, Australia's coral life, YouTube, the entire gamut.

That is the only way to realize that Dharma, the Buddha's teachings, alone is the truth; all else is chimera. "And you think we know nothing beyond the tenets of Buddhism," the lama said, chuckling. He seemed to mock me. I was mortified. My husband must have been embarrassed. Whatever the reason, a hush fell. We were all grappling with our ruminations.

In a few moments we reached the fabled 15th-century Tango Goemba. Perched on the edge of a cliff, it was stunning, frescoes and all. But my mind was elsewhere. In the short time we had spent there, I had fallen hopelessly in love with Bhutan.

Everything about it was differently similar to my homeland — the charming houses of slate and stone with colorful frescoes and painted phalluses, the cascading streams and ancient wooden bridges, the beautiful people with their warmth and grace, the tidy roads devoid of traffic signals, the *tsechu* (annual festival) with masked dancers and jesters, the women with their immense femininity and *khiras* (the traditional gown), the cuisine with its cheese and chilies, and the history, culture, tradition. I was at once at home and abroad. But it was here that I discovered the truth about myself.

The lama, half my age, knew so much about the world even while renouncing it. And here I was, priding myself on being educated, yet living with blinkers, prejudices and distorted biases. So, who was the one who had really renounced the world?

At 38, I took my first baby steps toward embracing — really, truly embracing — the world. I had been taught a valuable lesson. Not so much about Buddhism as about myself.

I can't imagine climbing up all the way to Tango ever again to scout out my lama friend, philosopher and guide. Maybe I should send a thank-you note to Kareena instead. After all, it was the love for her that serendipitously inspired the tale.

In another lifetime, Shilpa Gupta was a journalist being paid to write. She now is a traveler who writes, pay no bar. She and her husband have taken more than 20 holidays in the past two years and expect to shatter that record in the next two. However, she still hasn't figured out if she is a hill person or a sea person. Maybe she is a bit of both.

SAINTS AND SEA MONSTERS
Sicily

I arrived at the seaport windblown and disheveled, trying to channel the spirit of Ulysses and feel at one with his epic struggle. My own passage between Scylla and Charybdis had been less eventful than his, no doubt. But I had suffered the monsters' wrath nonetheless, as my ferryboat had tossed about in the Straits of Messina like a toy in the bathtub. It was late March and a strong Sirocco had swept up from Africa, bringing with it an angry current.

My queasy stomach lurched as I walked down the pier, but I was starving. I found a small bakery only a few hundred meters away and decided that a simple loaf of bread was probably the safest bet. I bounded through the front door impetuously while wrestling to remove my heavy backpack. However, my legs seemed convinced that we were still at sea — a sudden wave of vertigo threw me headfirst into the glass display case. The glass survived the collision but my dignity did not, as I splayed out across the floor like a drunken sailor.

A moment later (two seconds or two minutes, I'm not sure), a gentle hand on my shoulder roused me back to reality. The concerned face of an old woman hovered over me, although I couldn't quite determine if her concern was for my health or her display case.

It took me awhile to summon my Italian, but eventually I squeaked out a heartfelt apology. *"Mi dispiace, Signora, sono imbranato!"* I'm sorry, ma'am, I'm so clumsy!

Hearing my words, she offered only a hesitant smile and then I recalled that many older folks in Sicily spoke only their local dialect and weren't totally comfortable with standard Italian — especially when sullied by a thick American accent. To my great surprise, not only did she speak perfect Italian, but pretty decent English too.

"No problem, mister, do you feel fine?"

I was fine. Embarrassed, but fine. She helped me up off the floor and led me to a tiny table in the back of her store where she sat me down and gave me a glass of fizzy water with a slice of lemon. She stepped away for a moment, then returned with a dish of almond cookies and placed them in front of me as she sat down too.

"Mangi, mangi!" she exclaimed, as if I needed the encouragement.

As I munched, I perused the environs and noticed that there was nobody else in the little shop. It certainly wasn't a busy place, but I couldn't imagine that this 70-something-year-old woman could manage it by herself. I glanced at her wedding ring and for some reason blurted out, "*È sposata, signora?*" Are you married, ma'am?

She paused, then spoke in English, "My husband is died. Twelve year ago, is gone." Not exactly sadness in her voice, more like a detached nostalgia as she stared at the wall.

I followed her gaze and spotted a faded black and white photo of a man leaning against a horse cart, wearing a coppola hat and smoking a cigarette. Her husband, I assumed. I couldn't be too certain of this choppy, bilingual conversation, so I just nodded sympathetically and shoved another cookie in my mouth.

At last, her remedy was working — my spinning head had slowed down and the nausea was receding. I felt like I could breathe normally again, and my thoughts soon cleared.

******

What was I doing in Sicily, anyway? I had been living in Rome for more than two years, and began to feel like the capital city wasn't quite Italian enough for me anymore. I wanted a more intense experience, and all accounts had assured me that I'd find exactly that on the other side of The Straits. Goethe wrote, "To have seen

Italy without having seen Sicily is to not have seen Italy at all, for in Sicily lies the key to everything." I wanted to find out for myself what he meant.

My life in Rome had become a stagnate routine of short-term jobs and expat parties. In the historical center, it can often seem like you hear more English spoken than Italian. Every other night I was at an Irish pub watching a soccer match, or participating in a silly trivia contest in the hopes of winning a free bottle of scotch.

During the day I taught English, the default career choice for many expats in Italy. It paid the bills — barely. But it was repetitive and soulless, and left no room for optimism for career advancement. During one summer month of idleness, I had impulsively sent out dozens of job applications in the hopes of winning the lottery, so to speak. Long-term job contracts for foreigners in Italy almost don't exist. I wasn't holding my breath, but patted myself on the back for giving it a try.

In short, I was restless and I didn't really know what to do other than set out on a small adventure as a path to finding inspiration. Sicily had worked for Goethe and many other writers. Maybe it would work for me, too.

*****

A minute passed without either of us saying anything until finally the old woman let out a deep sigh and slumped back in her chair. Then without prompting she began to speak, telling me her life story as if it had been on the tip of her tongue for days, maybe years, waiting impatiently for the captive audience whom she had just found in me. She spoke mostly in broken English, but inserted a few words of Italian or Sicilian whenever her vocabulary was taxed.

She was only 5 years old in 1943 when the Allied bombs fell on Messina, killing her entire family along with thousands of other civilians. The nuns took her in, as they did with so many other war orphans. They cared for her, educated her, and became her new family. She wasn't obliged to join their order, but she was expected to do her share of the work, which she gratefully performed without complaint.

The sisters were typically strict and reluctant to allow her out in public unescorted. But as she got a little older, she was occasionally sent into town to buy food and other supplies for the convent. During one of these excursions, she began to take notice of a young man following her at a distance. He was a nice-looking boy, but his attentions made her uneasy.

Day after day he followed her through town, moving in a little closer each time. She'd catch him peeking at her through the garden fence. One day as she was walking home, he approached a little too closely and she got spooked. Luckily, as she rounded a corner, she spotted the church of St. Anthony, where she quickly dashed inside, hiding, and then knelt down in front of a statue of the famous saint and started to pray.

She prayed in earnest that St. Anthony would protect her from this relentless stalker —and, if he did, she vowed to marry a man named Anthony one day to show her gratitude. When she got back to the convent that afternoon, she found a painting of St. Anthony and hung it in her bedroom as a constant reminder. She prayed to him every day without fail. And her prayers were answered.

For the next several months her trips into town were uneventful — that menacing lad had miraculously vanished. So whenever she had a chance, she would stop back into the church to thank the blessed St. Anthony for answering her prayers, and to renew her promise to him.

About two months before her 18th birthday, she was on her way to the market again, as usual. She was picking through some tomatoes when she was startled by the sudden appearance of a young man practically standing in her shadow. She spun around and they were face to face. It was that same boy who had tracked her all over town several months before. This time he had been quick and sneaky, sidling up to her before she had a chance to escape.

He threw out his cigarette, removed his coppola hat, and introduced himself. His name was Anthony. They were married a year later.

*****

Her story stuck with me for some reason — just because we can't escape our fate doesn't mean that we shouldn't try. The value is in the struggle, and so when we finally arrive at our pre-destined terminus, we are better off for the trials that we've endured. At least that's what I told myself, and it was somehow reassuring. But it still didn't give me the answers that I had come to Sicily to find.

Back in my hotel room, I connected my laptop to the Internet and checked my e-mail. I had a message from a private university in Milan offering me a contract position as a *lettore*, a "reader" of English for the university students. The job is actually more prestigious than it sounds, and carries with it full professor privileges. I only vaguely remembered applying for the job six or seven months before, and had totally put it out of my mind, like the 50 or so other applications I had sent out in desperation.

It was a great offer, and six months ago I would have jumped at it. But now I wasn't sure if I wanted to opt for a life on the opposite side of the "Italian-ness" scale. If Rome had become too dull, imagine life in Milan!

I thought about it for a day, and then wrote back to the university asking for a week to consider their offer. I shoved my clothes, laptop and other items into my luggage. I checked out of the hotel, rented a car and set off to discover the rest of the island; that fabled kingdom of Gods and heroes, of poets and sea monsters, forever existing somewhere between myth and reality. I wanted to dive into the deep end.

The Sicilians claim that their ancient Trinacria (three-point island) was born from a precious gem, fallen from the crown of the Lord. Religion, legend and superstition are never far apart in Sicily. Long ago, a humble fisherman's son named Colapesce was diving in the waters off of Messina. While underwater, he noticed that the column of Pelora, on which the northern cusp of Sicily leans, was cracked and ready to crumble.

Fearing that at any moment his beloved Messina might sink, he stayed down there — transforming into half-man, half-fish — to support the pillar on his own shoulders. Nowadays, when the island experiences seismic tremors, it's said that Colapesce is merely readjusting his position to get comfortable.

Comfortable — good for him. I soon discovered that comfort is one thing that's in short supply in Sicily. The roads are terrible, the services unreliable and the infrastructure non-existent. Businesses close at random hours, and nobody seems to know the traffic laws, especially the police. The simplest everyday tasks often require a monumental degree of patience and stamina. I began to realize that the "simple life" in Sicily was not so simple after all, and my frustrations quickly began to mount, setting me on edge.

Five days into my road trip I stopped at Agrigento to see the famous Valley of the Temples, the best collection of Greek ruins anywhere, including Greece. My camera was recently equipped with a new lens, and I couldn't wait. But then, after parking my car, I arrived at the main entrance only to find the ticket booth closed.

A sign, handwritten in Italian, implored me to try the secondary entrance down the road. I had already paid to park my car in a lot, so I walked — about a mile — to the secondary entrance, only to be told that they don't take credit cards, only at the main entrance, which, of course, was closed. So I walked all the way back to my car and drove 15 minutes into the center of town to withdraw 50 euros at the ATM. Nearly an hour later, I arrived back at the secondary entrance and emphatically slapped my 50 euro banknote on the counter.

The employee looked at the bill, then looked up at me. He blinked once and said dryly, "*Mi dispiace, signore, non posso accettarlo. Non c'è il resto.*" Sorry, sir, I can't accept that. I don't have change.

I was thinking back to the old woman, and my own conclusions that "the value is in the struggle," and so on, which now sounded like utter nonsense. Cheap philosophical BS. Instead I was grateful for the thick glass that separated my fist from the man's face. I knew it wasn't solely his fault; he was merely the last in a long line of people determined to make my life as aggravating as possible since arriving on the island.

It was at about this time that I reluctantly admitted that Sicily was a bit too Italian for me. In fact, once I thought about it, maybe Rome was, too, and Milan couldn't possibly be that much better.

The old woman wanted to marry a saint, and instead ended up marrying the man she was trying to avoid. The irony was not lost on me. I had come to Sicily to drown myself in Italian culture, and instead discovered that I was too American to transform myself into something else, not as able to adapt as the heroic Colapesce.

By the time I got back to my apartment in Rome I had decided that it was time to go home. Back to the only place that I can truly call home. The next day I booked a flight and started packing my things. Saying *"arrivederci"* to Roma would be difficult. But not as difficult as living a life that I wasn't supposed to live, regardless of how appealing it appeared in myths and dreams.

Rick Zullo is an award-winning travel writer living between Rome and South Florida. When he's not wandering through Italy or writing for his blog, he spends his time studying Italian, trying to become fully fluent before his infant daughter beats him to it. He is also the author of the eBook, "Live Like an Italian," available on Amazon. Visit Rick's blog at rickzullo.com, or connect with him on Facebook or Twitter

HOUSE AT THE END OF THE ROAD
Chile

My tent squats low on a gravel bar. Its green nylon contrasts sharply with the surrounding vegetation. The tent fly flaps gently while I tie a new fly on.

I consider how hard it's been to reach this spot in Chile. It had taken days, including rides on two airplanes, two buses and a boat, plus two overnight stays and several hours of hiking, carrying a damnably heavy pack up through this exquisite valley. As the rod begins to load with the motions of the day's first casts, it looks like it has been well worth the trouble.

The sun shines, struggling to melt the ice and snow clinging to the peaks above. The valley is stunning. That sky! This stream! Those mountains! It's easy enough to imagine that no one has ever been up on those peaks.

There are no footprints through that snow, summer though it is.

The river is cold, pure, deep. It sings a lovely song. When the light is right and a current window opens, I can see trout holding behind the boulders.

The only footprints I saw on the trail were made by horses, sheep and cattle. The last house I passed, a lovely little cottage surrounded by fuscia and foxgloves, is miles behind me. I have seen no one. I again cast my woolly worm into the unfished stream, in this apparently uninhabited valley. I think to myself that in all likelihood these fish have never seen a fly before.

I enjoy the repetitious rhythm of cast-drift-mend, cast-drift-mend, interrupted occasionally by a strike. The browns are slightly more sluggish than the rainbows, but both fish are wild creatures, fat, strong and stunningly beautiful. They gaze at me piercingly as I hold and un-hook them. They seem relieved when they are placed back into the water. So far they've all been pretty aver-age, size-wise, but I am looking forward optimistically to hooking a 5-pounder.

Heck, why stop at 5? A 10-pounder, even better. Un-pressured, unsophisticated fish, in a river like this, pouring into the nearby sea, there must be scads of 10-pound trout here. I want one!

Suddenly, a shout comes from behind me. *Hola! Como esta?* Startled, I whip around to see what this invasion of my private Nirvana might mean. It's a rider, a young man, sitting on a large and very fast-looking horse, not six feet away. I had not heard them approach over the song of the river.

De donde es Usted? he asks. "Where are you from?" he wants to know.

Soy Americano. Estoy aqui para pescar. "I'm an American. I came here to fish," I answer. And I think to myself, "And you just scared the hell out of me. Could you go away now and let me fish, please?"

I want my solitude to come back. But the rider is not done with me, oh no.

He wants to converse. But my Spanish isn't good, and I want to fish. There is a 10-pound trout here somewhere, and I want to find it. My time is short. So with all due respect, Mr. Horseman, could you go away, right now, please?

No. He wants to converse. Although I don't understand much of what he says, one thing I do understand is that a good-sized chunk of this valley is the property of he and his brother, and I am trespassing on it. So I stand there quietly, uncertain what to say or do next.

Mi nombre es Hernan Fernandez. Mi hermano esta en Puerto Montt. Megusta Usted dormir en mi casa esta noche. Said with a smile.

I stand there silent for a moment, dumbfounded. Then some semblance of manners creeps into my consciousness, and I walk over and shake his hand. I hear myself saying, *Mucho gusto, Hernan, e muchas gracias.*

This is my reward for trespassing. I've just been invited to spend the night in the home of Hernan Fernandez.

It causes a dilemma, though. I don't want to spend the night in his home. I don't want to be an ambassador. I want to fish. I want to spend another night in my tent, in my sleeping bag. I want to fish again tomorrow morning before I have to leave. My mind races as I try to think of a diplomatic way to turn down his generous offer. None comes. Like it or not, I am spending the night at Chez Hernan.

He left then. I thought for a moment maybe I'd just stay where I was. But he soon came back with his fishing tackle — a small silver spinner tied to a length of monofilament, wrapped around a tin can. We fish together for a while, me with my fly rod, he with his can, from two different worlds, not saying much, catching and killing a few trout. They aren't quite as unfished as I had thought.

Hernan cleans the fish at the river's edge. He gives me directions to his house, then leaves. After a few moments I reluctantly pack my sleeping bag, strike the tent and break down my tackle. I hoist my backpack, and go looking for this house at the end of the earth.

Hernan is lighting two kerosene lamps when I arrive. He gives me a tour of his home. It doesn't take long. There are only two rooms, very Spartan. One room has a beautiful wood stove, a handmade table and two handmade wooden chairs. The obligatory calendars featuring naked women hang, two for each wall. The other room has two beds. From the rafters hang every kind of tack imaginable — saddles, bridles, collars, reins, hobbles, buckets, ropes, and a whole lot of other farming-looking stuff with which I am totally unfamiliar.

The house is small, and clean enough, and warm, and nicely lit. It looks altogether like quite a nice place to live, as long as you don't need a TV and a dishwasher and all that sort of thing. I still want to be in my tent, but the feeling is starting to soften a bit.

It is getting dark. We are both hungry. We sit down at the table. Hernan takes out some bread and butter and cheese. I supply peanut butter and honey and dried fruit. As we eat a simple dinner he tells me he and his brother are farmers. He is 17 years old. His brother is 21. They have 16 cows, and horses, goats, sheep, various fowl, a garden, pasture, woods and, of course, the river.

He wants to know about me. I tell him I am an American. I live in Brazil, and I am a schoolteacher there. I have come to this valley on my summer vacation to fly fish for trout. I intend to hike back to Bariloche.

I have enough trouble conversing in English. This language barrier is altogether too big. It is very hard work holding up my end of the conversation.

As we talk and eat, dusk comes on. Inside the house it begins to rain ants.

At first there are only a few. But as it gets darker the ants become more numerous, big ones, flying around and crawling on everything. They become impossible to ignore.

Hernan says, *Estes formigos san muy perigosos*. Certain that I have misunderstood him, I ask him to repeat himself. *Mas despacio, por favor*. "More slowly, please." He repeats himself, word for word, very slowly and very clearly. There is no mistaking his meaning. "These ants are very dangerous."

I want to know why. He says, in Spanish, "They crawl into your ear."

I know a little entomology. I teach biology. I have never before heard of ants taking refuge in a human ear. As an American ambassador to this man's home I can't tell him he doesn't know what he's talking about. So I ask him diplomatically if he knows anyone this has happened to.

Si, un chico, abajo el valle. "Yes, a little boy down the valley." "What happened to him?" I want to know. "The ant had to be removed surgically," he says.

I am trapped by good manners and circumstance in a small house full of large flying ants that want to eat their way into my brain. It's a hell of a long way to a doctor. I have a perfectly good tent that will keep the ants off of me, out of my ears. The accursed aforementioned good manners prevent me from using it. I grit my teeth, and resolve to make the best of the situation.

Hernan and I finish dinner with somewhat diminishing conversation. All my brain power is being used to wonder how I'm going to keep the ants out of my ears. There's not enough brain left to translate too.

After dark, without electricity, Hernan and his brother always go to bed early. They're farmers, and their long days start at dawn. I soon find myself preparing to lie down in the brother's bed.

The bed, to my surprise and relief, is absolutely heavenly. The sheets are clean, even though they're made out of flour sacks. The mattress, the comforter and the pillow are stuffed with goose down. It's like lying on a cloud, as delicious as a bed could be. But this cloud lacks a silver lining. This cloud is lined with ants.

All night long, every time I start to doze off, ants crawl on me. I awake with a start, and begin slapping. I can't sleep, afraid one will crawl into my ear. Then I don't feel one for a while, and exhausted from travel, hiking and fishing, I doze off again. Another ant wakes me, and the process repeats. Just to make things even more interesting, my throat is sore because I'm getting sick.

It's a slightly torturous infinite loop. Dawn is a long time coming.

Dawn does finally show. Except for the dead ones, of which there are plenty, the ants are gone. We eat some breakfast, bread and peanut butter and unpasteurized milk. I pack my belongings. I take some photos of Hernan. I thank him profusely for his hospitality. I shoulder my too-heavy backpack. We say goodbye.

I feel fortunate, surviving the ants. Thinking of the 10-pound trout I'm not going to find here, I begin the long walk back to Bariloche.

John Kumiski is a writer and photographer specializing in the outdoors and travel. He enjoys the challenges of trying to capture the beauty, the subtleties and the grandeur of nature. He makes his living selling writing and photography, and taking folks fishing. His work has won many awards and prizes. He lives in central Florida with his wife Susan and their two cats.

CALLING MY NAME IN MAASAI
Kenya

Kenya, April 2010

In a maze of dormitory bunk beds in Maasailand, Kenya, Mara inspects my arm freckles. She brushes her finger over my arm hair and traces my blue veins from the crook of my elbow to my wrist. I play: I search her arms and face for freckles. I find no freckles, no arm hair. No blue veins show through her dark skin.

She examines my blonde hair and plucks strays from my shirt. She holds each one up in the sunlight and giggles. I play: I pick hairs from myself and place them on her sweater, as if they were her blonde hairs.

"Do you want to be black like me?" Mara asks, in the middle of our game.

"Do *you* want to be white like *me?*" I ask.

"Yes," she says. Her voice rises as she smiles, but she fixes her gaze on the floor.

"Why?"

"Because you are beautiful."

"*You* are beautiful. I think the beauty is in our differences." I try to explain the age-old concept I have heard many times.

"It's like how people in America want to come to Kenya and people in Kenya want to come to America," I continue. "We want to go because it is different than what we know."

"Yes," she says, softer this time as she contemplates this idea.

She turns and chatters to her friends for a moment in a language I don't know, and then turns back to me.

"Silantoi," she says. "Your Maasai name. Silantoi."

I ask her what it means in English and she tells me: courageous.

I play with this Maasai word in my mind, asking her to repeat it so I won't forget. "Cilantro" is how I transpose it to English and commit it to memory; that and the stains of its black-ink letters written on my forearm by her. I wonder if I deserve acceptance from this Maasai girl. I wonder what I could have done to earn this honor. And, after she and her sisters tell me that morning how they came to be here at the Olooloitikoshi Girl's Rescue Center, I want to understand how Mara could ever deem me courageous.

Later, I find her standing close to the cool, outer brick walls of the dormitory, hiding in the shadows of the short bushes that skirt the buildings. Laundry hangs from the black chain-link fence of the rescue center and girls move around the compound, taking out the trash, tending the small garden, and washing dishes. Mara looks out over the plains beyond the fence of the rescue center, her fingers busy on the waxy surface of a leaf. Beyond the few structures around the GRC there are stretched-out plains and gentle hills, greener than anyone has seen them in years.

Shadows roll over the land; they are products of a big, open Wyoming-esque sky full of stacked cumulus clouds that sometimes spit rain in long, straight lines. That is what I see; I think Mara sees the vast space between herself and her younger sister, Ruth. Ruth is 10 and will undergo circumcision within the year if she doesn't leave home. The two sisters are close friends, only one year apart in age but far apart in circumstance.

Mara has the privilege of living at this rescue center, which means many things: a chance for education, three meals a day, clean water, the provision of basic necessities like clothes, and safety from the threat of circumcision and early marriage that most of the rescue center girls left home to avoid.

In Kenya, female circumcision — sometimes called female genital mutilation — has long been considered a rite of passage into womanhood, and signals readiness for marriage. The World Health Organization says that

"Female genital mutilation comprises all procedures involving partial or total removal of the external female genitalia or other injury to the female genital organs for non-medical reasons." WHO estimates that 100-140 million girls and women worldwide have been circumcised, with three million African girls at risk each year.

Women interviewed for the 2008-2009 Kenya Demographic and Health Survey stated some of the benefits were cleanliness, less promiscuity and better marriage prospects. Still, an average of 82 percent of Kenyan women ages 15 to 49 said that female circumcision should be stopped.

In 2008-2009 WHO estimated a 27 percent prevalence rate of female circumcision in Kenya overall. But the prevalence rate was 73 percent in the Maasai tribe, which many of the GRC girls, including Mara and her sisters, are a part of.

Mara is the third of 10 children: two boys and eight girls. In a patriarchal society, the girls are of value to their father as they reach puberty and can be circumcised and sold into marriage, alleviating their father of school and living costs and rewarding him with dowry cows. Indeed, tradition and cows — which sustain the semi-nomadic lifestyle of many Maasai men — are two reasons that early marriage continues, says Joseph Mure Orket who, for 18 years, was the chief of Kenya's Kajiado District, where the GRC is.

Orket visits the rescue center frequently. His Mercedes SUV rocks slowly toward the center, up the only road that reaches it. His car is clean, and the sun glints off its silver veneer. He looks dignified, dressed in khakis and a striped, collared shirt with the top button undone, and has a shy smile that creeps out every now and then. He describes himself as a "seer of the future," and the link between the community and the government.

With the help of educational programs, nongovernmental organizations, government programs and churches, some local leaders, like Orket, are trying to change the mentality about female circumcision. Currently in Maasai culture, men cannot marry an uncircumcised girl and girls can beg to be circumcised because it makes them feel mature. This mentality, he says, is sure to change with education and time.

Despite these efforts, and the fact that female circumcision is illegal in Kenya, rural girls are still not well-protected. Many leave their homes and families to escape circumcision. Those who escape may find refuge at the house of a relative, local chief or pastor. When girls report their situations at home to local authorities, their cases are submitted to the Department of Children Services at the Ministry of Gender, Children, and Social Development.

Subsequently, some girls apply for a sponsorship at centers like the Olooloitikoshi Girl's Rescue Center, which is where I'm spending two weeks with the Colorado couple that helped establish it.

One day I am in the rescue center's guard shack for the second time with Mara and Tina, one of the center's founders. We carry three blue, plastic chairs from the crowded dining room across a muddy field to the guard shack, where we all cram in for privacy. I set my small video camera on the table and Mara shies away. She is less at ease inside these cinder block walls than outside with her friends. I learn that she hasn't yet shared her full story with anyone except the Kenyan police.

The first time I heard about female circumcision was six months earlier from a white, American man. I don't remember my reaction. It was October 2009, halfway through my newspaper reporting internship at the Greeley Tribune, and I interviewed Mark, one of the center's founders. As a young journalist trying to be objective at all moments of covering any story, I imagine myself stone-faced in front of him, nodding curiously. That issue and those girls were, as the saying goes, a different world.

"You should come with us sometime," Mark said at the end of our interview about the GRC. He and his wife Tina, along with their church and Christian Mission Aid in Kenya, were building the GRC. "Come see the work we're doing in Kenya."

I opened my mouth, speechless for only a second.

"I would love to," I told him.

A month later, Mark called me with an invitation to Kenya; I was to write a couple of newspaper stories while there. And now I'm here.

In the guard shack at the GRC, I try to ignore my churning stomach as Mara tells me her story.

She is the most recent escapee of her household, and she left two days before her scheduled circumcision. Years earlier she saw both of her older sisters, Eve and Faith, held down by women in their town and circumcised against their will. But they were silent; they did not yell for help, she says.

After multiple failed attempts to escape from home, from impending arranged marriages, and from a father who would beat his children often, her two older sisters finally left home for good and were brought to the GRC together; Tina and I had learned this in an earlier interview with Eve, Faith and Mara.

"You saw all of this," Tina says to Mara. "All of this was going on around you. How did you feel about everything?"

There is a long pause. Mara scuffles her flip-flops on the cement floor; it sounds like sandpaper on wood. She smiles, and looks at me. She doesn't understand the question. I suspect no one ever asked her how she felt about anything. We all laugh for a minute, and then her expression drops.

"What?" she asks. Tina tries again. Eventually, we are able to put together her story.

Knowing she would soon face circumcision and marriage, she had confided in a teacher, who told her to run away when the time was right. Two months after her two oldest sisters escaped, Mara, Ruth and their brother David were left at home with their father. Mara woke in the night to her father staring down at her body. He had stripped off all her clothes. She told her father that she was taking her younger siblings to the outdoor bathroom. After she locked him in the house, Mara left with her two younger siblings. She slept at a teacher's house, and left her siblings in the morning.

When she went to the road to catch a bus to her great-uncle's house, she ran into a neighbor who paid for her to get there after she told him of the escape. Ruth and David were found and taken back to their father's home. Mara spent two months at her great-uncle's before she was brought to the GRC.

When I think about Mara, I think about all of this. But I also think about a childhood song that she sang into my video camera one afternoon.

"Cecelia, sing with me," she said first. Then:

"I want to dance like this, so deep down in my heart.

"I want to jump like this, so deep down in my heart.

"So deep, deep, so down, down. So deep down in my heart."

In the recording I hear her breathlessness and the crunchy gravel beneath her feet as she sings and bounces around in showing me the song. In the moment of play, as I laugh behind the camera, we both seem to have forgotten the reality of the stories she told me about herself, her sisters, her life.

"You look up at the sky and think of me," I say when she was nearly in tears on the day I'm leaving. "And I'll do the same. We have the same sky."

The sky is the only thing I can think of that can visually bridge our ever-changing lives without freezing us in a moment, like a video or picture does. Every day we both see the sky, I reason; every day we can both see a bit of each other there. It is the most tangible thing as I leave her for my home, half a world away.

Colorado 2010-2011

I am at the GRC, and a girl prances and plays around me. I look down at her in shock. She is petite and blonde, a miniature me. I am in disbelief at the sight of her; I hug her and touch her as if she is an apparition, unreal in some way even before my eyes. But I know that's not the case. She is the fourth sister, Ruth. When the scene finally startles me awake, I am crying in my basement room in Colorado.

A couple months later, at a reunion for people who have worked on the GRC project, I introduced myself to the woman who coordinates education sponsorships for the GRC girls. My family started sponsoring a girl and I wanted to find out more about her. I had only an inkling that we were sponsoring the little girl from my dream.

I knew Ruth needed a sponsor to be taken from her home and upcoming circumcision, and I knew that had happened the summer after I was in Kenya. With the realization that my family, almost 9,000 miles away, played a part in reuniting Mara with her little sister, I cried and smiled and tried to control myself.

My curiosity about what these sisters, and all the GRC girls, faced became insatiable. I searched for stories about women who underwent circumcision or were threatened by early marriage. In my university library, I found mostly works by anthropologists and slogged through them. I interviewed people who work with girls in Kenya who are threatened by early marriage and female circumcision. I used school projects and research paper assignments as excuses to write about female circumcision. During my last year of college, I worked restaurant jobs and saved my pennies for a return trip to Kenya.

College graduation came and went, but my craving for Kenya was still strong. At a GRC fundraiser late in 2011, Tina handed me her cell phone and told me to scroll through her gallery to find a video greeting from Mara.

I ran my finger over the touch screen, through a blur of Tina's pictures, and clicked on a few videos before finding the one she told me about. There was Mara facing the camera. As the fundraiser rolled on around me, I brought the phone closer to my ear to hear her saying hello, hoping that my family and I were well, and hoping I could come back to Kenya.

*****

Kenya, April 2012

I spot Mara immediately, at the front of church. She is caught up in worship song and dance with a group of GRC girls. If she sees me she doesn't let on. Her eyes never meet mine or glance toward my video camera. Before she acknowledges me, I take her in. She is not a little girl anymore, but a teenager. She is taller, with the breathtakingly beautiful figure of her two older sisters; her long limbs sway gracefully and her movements are gentle. She is enviably poised, and I see confidence in her as she dances. Ruth is next to her, a spitting image of Mara two years ago, but more timid. As soon as the song is over, Mara grabs my hand and leads me outside with the procession of girls.

"You came back! My friend," she keeps saying, throwing her arms around my shoulders. "I miss you."

"She is my friend," she tells Alex, my boyfriend.

"She's a good friend to have," he replies.

"She's my sister," Mara says.

I am happy and proud to be welcomed back by her; with her warm hand on my arm, I recall the ease of our friendship.

But that ease dissipates in the next couple of weeks, and she seems wary of me, nervous. I thought I would come back to the same childlike, free-spirited Mara that I left two years ago, but this is not the case. We don't talk and laugh and joke like we did before. She hardly speaks to me after that day outside the church, but would smile from a distance.

"You have changed so much since I last saw you," I tell her one day when we have a moment to talk in the hot GRC kitchen. "From a little girl who was always playing, to a teenage girl who is just so cool."

I changed, too, she says, laughing. I don't talk and joke as much. I realize how much pressure I had put on this trip: My goal was to come back to Kenya and interview her extensively to understand more of her story. But she politely refuses my informal requests to talk. I guiltily recall the sad eyes and furrowed brow that defined her face as she listened to a recent interview I had with her mother.

Our eyes met once during the interview, and there I saw a fear and disgust that made me feel ashamed for digging so deeply into her personal life. With only 30 minutes for the impromptu interview, I felt forced to jump right into questions about the girl's father.

I beamed and fought back tears the afternoon that Mara's mother came to the GRC. Except for one coincidental meeting in a nearby town, the girls hadn't seen her since they left home two years earlier. Faith, Mara and Ruth noticed her coming down the road in front of the GRC and hesitated briefly, unsure of whether they were allowed to leave the boundaries of the gate. Then they ran for her. Their mother brought two of the younger siblings along. One was David, the little brother that was with Mara and Ruth when they fled home. The other was a toddler, the eighth girl in the family. As they walked back toward the gates, they hugged and greeted each other and cried.

She greeted Tina and me at the gate with hugs, handshakes and thanks. It made sense that she would thank Tina, who helped give her girls a second chance, but I wasn't sure I deserved thanks. She exuded humility and deep gratitude just like her girls. They all looked alike, unmistakably family. But they smiled at us and she looked at the ground. When they reached the dining room Eve came out to join them. She greeted the three family members, and cried unabashedly. I recalled Eve's shyness and emotionless exterior from two years ago, and I couldn't help but cry also.

In the dorms before the interview, their mother held my hand for a long time as she spoke to me in a language I didn't understand: Maasai or Swahili, indistinguishable to my ears. When asked, I told her my name was Cece. When asked for my second name, I was unsure what to say.

"Silantoi," one of the GRC girls told her. It was the first time anyone had spoken my Maasai name since I came back, and I told her Mara gave it to me. It is a good name, she said.

When Mara pointed out the ways I had changed, I realized that more than wanting to be a journalist telling her story, I just wanted to be her silly friend again. I wanted to hug her and apologize for asking the hard questions. I wanted to cry with her. I really wanted her to see me as Silantoi, but I wasn't sure she did anymore.

*****

The scraping of the plastic chairs on the cement floor resonated through the dining room as Eve and I adjusted for an interview later that week. She looked me straight in the eye as she sat leaning on the edge of the table. She was smiley and animated, gesturing as she spoke. Despite the changes with Mara, I grew steadily closer to Faith and Eve on my second trip to Kenya. Once again, how much Eve had grown hit me hard. Two years before, Eve bore the burden of explaining to me her father's sexual tendencies and threats of marriage, and her and her sisters' attempts to escape from him. She had spoken at a nearly inaudible volume, with her eyes locked on the floor and her mouth drooping in what I thought was resignation.

Now she was confident in every question she answered. Again, she explained her life before the center: threatening encounters with her father, extended stays at the homes of relatives, school absences and her final success at being brought to the GRC with Faith.

In a burst of momentum, we reached a question that I asked almost every girl and woman I interviewed in Kenya. I paused while I thought about whether or not to ask it. Girls joked and yelped just outside the open windows, making happy noise as I quickly decided that now was the right time for the hardest question.

"Ummmm, is it OK if I ask, were you circumcised?"

"Yes," she replied quickly.

"How old were you?"

"I was 11."

"Did you and Faith have your circumcision together?"

"Yes."

I pressed on gently, unsure of whether she would stop me if things got too hard to talk about. In Maasai culture it is not custom to talk about the day of circumcision, and every time I asked the question during an interview I felt the tension rise. The trust between me and my past interview subjects wasn't there. I didn't blame them: I wouldn't discuss my female organs with strangers from halfway across the world either. But I had interviewed Eve before, as well as her sisters and her mother. She had told me difficult details of her home life twice now. I had been allowed entry, and I truly believed she trusted me as we went on.

"It was so bad because we were not taken to hospital. It was just a doctor came to our home. That woman, in the morning, and circumcised us," she said. "We are feeling so painful, and we are bleeding so badly."

I was quiet as I wrote her answer. My head was spinning with disbelief, but it wasn't because of what she was saying. I have read these facts. It's because Eve was the first female I asked that didn't shake her head and quietly refuse the question.

All the things I had read and heard became reality through this girl who, two years before, I never would have guessed would be the one to help me understand female circumcision on an intensely personal level. From what she told me, I could envision the day vividly.

Eve and Faith woke up early, ready to complete their daily tasks as the two oldest children in the family. They were told by their father that they would be circumcised within hours. Their mother pleaded, trying to convince him not to do it, but she was told that she had no authority in the family, so she kept quiet and their father went on with his plan to circumcise the girls in preparation for marriage.

The girls, too, were powerless. Sadness and panic rose in them. They were told by non-governmental organization workers at school that circumcision was bad. People die, they were told, because they bleed so much and cannot get to a hospital. Others live, but when the time comes for marriage and giving birth, they can feel so much pain because the part that used to expand during birth was cut, Eve told me. The NGO workers tried to talk to parents too, she said, but the parents refused the teachings and went on.

Neighboring women and children gathered in the family's two-bedroom hut, and the men were outside, awaiting the celebration that follows the procedure. Eve is the oldest, and she was circumcised first. She was laid down and women surrounded her, holding her hands and legs and covering her eyes and mouth. As the procedure began, she tried to scream, but could not. After 5 minutes it was over. The course of her life changed forever, and she thought about herself, she said.

"What can I do now?" she wondered. "I have already been circumcised."

But Eve kept quiet, because there was no one to help her, she said. Faith, one year younger, was next.

After the circumcision the community celebrated the girls' passage into womanhood with the slaughtering of two goats. During the celebration, Eve said she was not feeling happy or proud about their fresh circumcision. Both girls were sleeping in the house.

"In the afternoon, I tried to wake up to go outside. I fainted and I just find myself when I was lying on the floor and people are surrounding me," Eve told me. "I asked them what was happening and they told me I fainted. So, it was a hard way."

"How do you feel about all of this now?" I asked.

"Now? I just keep quiet and keep God to control me because I don't have any other ways now," she told me. She said many of the other girls at the GRC are not circumcised. "I used to feel very bad because I was circumcised at home but I didn't want it, to be circumcised, but because of my father that is why I am circumcised."

"Do you still feel so bad about it?"

She said simply, "Yes."

I told her that I think she will be successful, even though she is circumcised, because she is smart and good. She laughed and smiled and thanked me. But despite having just finished at the top of her class in primary school, she had her doubts about being successful in the future. I told her she seemed much happier than when I first met her, and I asked if she was feeling better. She assured me that she was.

Since Eve and her sisters came to the center in 2010, things have improved at home. Since my last visit, the girls have assured me that their father has changed. And when he visited them at the GRC in August 2013, he assured his four oldest daughters that everything would be OK.

After my interview with Eve, I was in a state of disbelief about her level of openness with me. Without her and her younger sisters, it seemed, there was a whole world out there that I never would have entered.

I thanked her, told her that I love her, and that she is like a sister to me.

"And me, I love you too," she said.

Colorado, June 2012

After spending two months in East Africa, culture shock at home worked in me subtly and gradually, with time. Once in a while, when I really stopped to think about it, I was shocked at the comparative ease and luxury of American life, at people who threw impatient fits in grocery store lines and traffic jams, at the realization that we can get anything we want at any time we want it in our country. I understood this shock to be typical, familiar, guilt-ridden. But most of the time I mulled. I tried to figure out how I could carry the heavy weight of difficult stories, true stories.

One night in Denver, Alex and I walked and talked about the oddities of culture shock, how it can be subtle and subconscious. How can I be lighthearted, I asked him. Sometimes, I think about the stories I've heard and my breath catches in my chest. How could I carry this suffocating weight? I no longer have the choice to be accidentally ignorant, as I was the first time I sat down with Mark and heard the words "female circumcision." I know about it now. I can't ignore it. I've heard about it firsthand. After our walk I poured myself a glass of Chianti. And another. And I got lost in my thoughts.

Finally, I understood Silantoi. I realized that, in Mara's eyes, it took courage for me to go to Kenya. Not the kind of courage required to eat strange food or speak another language, but the kind of courage required to enter deeply into the way other people live, to not ignore the sights and sounds and struggles of other humans. It takes courage to hear firsthand what it's like for a girl to be beaten and circumcised. It takes courage to forge a new friendship. It takes courage to try and understand this world. I admit to myself that I am a more troubled person after two trips to Kenya. Both times I boarded the plane to go there I was in it for fun and adventure, to learn new things and teach others about them. In my eyes this didn't make me the least bit courageous.

Maybe Mara called me Silantoi because I simply listened to her family's story and, by doing so, entered her world and endured a tiny fraction of the hardships and courage that she has. I didn't see myself that way, but perhaps she did. Rather, I would call her courageous because she told her story, and let an outsider into a world that an outsider can never truly understand. I recall her words in a letter to me:

"I think about you, my dear, when I look at the blue sky. We are together."

Cece Romanyshyn is a freelance writer and elementary school librarian in Fraser, Colorado. She has traveled in the United States, Costa Rica, Kenya, Tanzania and Ecuador, and writes about her travels at happilylostwithcece.wordpress.com. This story is a modified excerpt from her first self-published book, In the Place of Many Zebras. Learn more at intheplaceofmanyzebras.com.

OPEN EYES
USA

There are 32 pairs of teenage eyes on me, and I'm beginning to sweat. It's "Career Day" at Denver's Kennedy High School, and I'm speaking about my job as an international journalist.

So far, my speech hasn't gone too well. The young man in the back corner is asleep, and a girl in the front row is playing games on her cell phone. Most of the others have a glazed look in their eyes.

Desperate, I plunge on with my lecture, talking of assignments in Thailand, interviews in England and stories in Singapore.

But I may as well be speaking of the moon. For most of these students, the rest of the world is a far-off place. They have little exposure to it, and frankly, they're not all that interested.

And who can blame them? I once felt just like they do.

After all, when you grow up with limited exposure to other lands and ways of life, it can lead you to believe that the rest of the world is just like the one in which you grew up. So what reason is there to explore new places? I had little interest in other countries and cultures.

Then I met Melanie.

We all have people who come into our lives who influence or change us somehow. For me, one of those people was a 20-year-old girl from a farm town in Iowa.

I was attending college in Indiana that year, and I met Melanie on the school's softball team. In truth, we really didn't play much, but sat out game after game with injuries. While our team sailed on to victories (without us, no doubt), Melanie and I sat on the bench and talked. We eventually became roommates.

Melanie was different from anyone I had ever known. She made me laugh with her witty sense of humor, but most of all, she was a story teller. Her tales were different though, for she had been outside of the country.

Day after day, she weaved stories of places I had never imagined. She talked of dreamy Austrian villages and narrow, ancient streets. She told of tall, handsome Dutch boys and the thrill of cruising down the German autobahns.

At first, I feigned disinterest, but eventually I began to listen, picturing this world that she painted with words. Eventually, like Chinese water torture, Melanie wore me down.

"OK!" I said one evening after a long story regaling the thrills of travel. "I give up! I want to see this for myself. Let's go!"

And so we did.

Culture shock set in as soon as we stepped foot in Amsterdam on that week-long trip during semester break. Surrounded by the staccato sounds of Dutch, I felt like a fish out of water. I wanted to rush back into the plane and head for the familiarity of home.

But I was stuck here, so I followed Melanie through the streets of Rotterdam. She laughed and talked with everyone she met, not afraid of the new things she saw. Slowly, I began to view this new world through her eyes. My discomfort turned to curiosity and then interest.

We spent New Year's Eve in Rotterdam, and I watched in awe as the local residents poured into the streets that night, lighting monstrous fireworks, drinking warm drinks and greeting each other (and me!) with two-cheeked kisses.

Right then, even though I couldn't understand a word being spoken around me, I smiled with glee. Mars had turned into heaven on earth.

From there, Melanie and I rented a little Peugeot and headed out through Europe. We fumbled our way through the countryside, getting lost, but always stopping to ask cute boys for directions. We ran into difficulties with the new languages and cultures, of course, but Melanie just laughed and considered it an adventure.

We drove through Holland and Germany, but it was Austria that broke down any resistance I had to accepting new cultures. The beauty of the Alps surrounding Salzburg took my breath away, and in the cozy cafés that are such an integral part of Austrian culture, I discovered a never-before-seen side of myself. I learned the quiet joy of sitting all afternoon around a tiny table, drinking dark coffee with whipped cream and discussing questions of life with new friends.

Perhaps that is why we are drawn to travel, for in leaving our homes and venturing into other parts of life, it reveals a side that we would never discover otherwise. In learning about others, we learn most about ourselves.

Vienna was the last straw for me. Wandering with Melanie and my new Austrian friends at midnight down the cobblestone streets of this former imperial city, I could barely contain my delight. Something, I knew, had awakened deep inside of me.

Nine months after that first trek to Europe, I packed up my college boxes and moved to Austria, where I attended university before eventually returning home to the States. My life had turned down a whole new path.

Sadly, that path didn't include Melanie. She graduated and became a teacher. True to her love of adventure, she chose to work in a whole new city and culture — San Antonio.

My fascination with exploring other cultures and destinations never left me. I became a journalist, and then
an editor with an international travel magazine.

For almost a decade, Melanie and I lost touch. Then
one day a colleague asked me the question: "Why did
you choose this career path?"

I immediately saw an image of Melanie, chatting
over dinner at the college cafeteria, telling me stories of
worlds I had never known. It was time to track down my
long-lost friend.

That evening, I looked up Melanie's parents on the
Internet. They were still living on their farm in Iowa. My
former roomie had gone on to become a principal, turning entire schools around with her passion for success
and achievement. I grinned as I dialed her number.

With some friends, lost years just slip away and
you're right back to your same relationship. That was
how it was with Melanie. Within minutes, she had me
laughing as we talked. Life was going well and my
friend was very successful. "But I really miss having the
chance to travel," she admitted.

So we remedied that. Each year, we meet up somewhere in the world and spend a week exploring. Last
year it was the Scottish Isles; next year it will be Swit-
zerland. Who knows where we'll end up next?

Melanie is the reason I am standing in front of this
classroom today. So I stop my speech, take a deep breath
and try another angle. Forget stories of journalism; there
are better tales to tell.

I begin to talk of Dutch celebrations, of dreamy Austrian villages and the thrill of cruising down the German autobahn. And in the back corner, I see something stir. The boy in the back has woken up, and I can't help but grin.

After all, it takes just one person to open your eyes to the world.

Janna Graber is a travel writer, editor and producer. Her writing has appeared in national publications including Chicago Tribune, The Denver Post, Reader's Digest, Parade, Redbook and Alaska Airlines. She is an editor at Go World Travel Magazine (GoWorldTravel.com), an international publication covering the world's most fascinating people and places. Follow her at @AColoradoGirl

A LIGHT IN THE DARKNESS
Cambodia

This is a story of faith.

Several years ago in a cave, in a ruin, in a Cambodian jungle, I spent less than an hour with a female hermit who has impacted my life to this day.

I have always considered my travels to be a learning process and have sought out those small crumbs on the path of enlightenment, dropped by those who preceded me, taking bits and pieces from each belief and forging them into my own.

On my first trip to Cambodia I spent much of my time deep in the jungles with Buddhist monks, most of whom welcomed me as a seeker, but I found many of them to be far more worldly than anticipated.

I had always seen women at the monasteries and ignorantly assumed them to be housekeepers or servants. I only learned they were nuns through a very unique experience.

A local guide was driving me through the jungle to a remote temple when we were stopped by one of the numerous freelance soldiers left over from Khmer Rouge days. In the countryside of Asia there are more than a few of these guys, former military, down on their luck, who make their living shaking down people like me who venture a bit too far off the beaten path.

I had just handed him some money when a tiny woman appeared, it seemed, from out of nowhere. She barely came up to my shoulder and had a shaved head, wore a white blouse, black drawstring pants, and was barefoot. Her milky eye was sightless and her grin was missing a few teeth but this did not stop her from thrusting her alms bowl between me and the startled soldier.

We were both taken off guard by her silent appearance, and I fumbled for a couple bills that I dropped into her bowl while the soldier was apparently so ashamed of being caught in his actions toward me that he gave her part of the bribe I had just paid him. The woman turned and, without saying a word, disappeared into the jungle. As the soldier waved me on he spat in her direction and said "Yiyay Chi" which I later found out was Khmer for nun. She was the first one I encountered.

The jungles of Cambodia are filled with ornate shrines, massive stone edifices with larger than life stone-carved Buddhas, colorful prayer flags, incense burners and candles, all in danger of being reclaimed by the jungle. Each is manned by a praetorian guard of chattering monkeys, spitting cobras, saffron-robed monks and nuns. They dot the remote countryside, surviving off the largesse of trekkers and pilgrims in the most unlikely places; small islands of beauty in a land devastated by 2,000 years of war.

I spent long hours in conversation with the monks at these temples, oftentimes talking well into the night of all things both spiritual and temporal and usually came away in awe of these simple jungle dwellers, most of whom had no formal education and yet were so fervent in their beliefs and happy in their lives as to make me question my own sense of purpose. I also noticed that during these times the nuns would fade into the background, sweeping, tending to candles or incense, serving tea, always busy but with downcast eyes, and never looking in my direction.

I was told that most of them were either poor or widows and, lacking the means to remain in the material world, had entered the spiritual one to build karma in their final years for the life that was to follow. I came to believe they might outnumber the monks, but were simply overshadowed by the colorful robes and more outgoing personalities.

I began to seek them out, intentionally making eye contact and eventually gaining a slight smile from more than one, but whenever I tried to begin a conversation most of them would put a finger to their mouth and signal me to silence. I took this to mean their commitment to another place was total and they had no time to give to outside visitors.

Compared to the monks, who for the most part wore civilian clothing on their free time and liked to smoke cigarettes and frequent local bars if only for sodas, the nuns seemed more focused on things spiritual. None of them passed along any revealing esoteric dogma, but I believe my attraction to them was born out of their simplicity and aura of serenity.

In my travels throughout the country I had avoided going to Angkor, knowing it to be an anthill of tourists, surpassing in popularity even the Great Wall of China. Through a friend's efforts, I finally entered the complex early one morning before the tide of humanity, and alone, made my way to Prasat Bayan, the center of Angkor Thom, former capital of the Khmer ruler, Jayavarman V11, the Mahayana Buddhist king, and famous for its 216 gigantic carved stone faces.

I was wandering alone through one of mankind's great artistic achievements, marveling at the craftsmanship that produced these monuments so long ago without modern technology and musing about how one small section of just one face could be the entire life's work of a single person. The Khmer carved stone like most people breathe and they imparted a soul to it. The entire history of the Khmer civilization is preserved in stone at the Angkor complex, a gigantic hand-carved book for the world to read.

That morning I watched a small girl climb the side of a temple face with a shawl full of fruit under her arm, and just before nearing the top she disappeared. I waited and watched to see the girl emerge from somewhere on the rock face hidden to me from below, and when she reached the ground I asked what she was doing. She just pointed up and said, "The lady."

Those words chilled me and now often return in my dreams, followed by her face.

I began to make my way up the ancient stone wall, finding small makeshift altars along the way where people had left behind burned candles, offerings of food, and even a photo of what I assumed was a deceased relative. Suddenly, just above me, a tiny face peered over the edge. She had short white hair and an enigmatic Mona Lisa smile. She was a hermit nun. Her face was a roadmap of hard times and yet her age was indecipherable. She radiated peace.

Cresting the ledge I found her seated on a stone slab in a smoke-filled cell that most likely had been occupied for prayer and meditation for centuries. There was no furniture or bed, nor was there room for any. She was clothed all in muslin with a shawl over her shoulder, spotless in her closet-like cell. Her eyes touched me like fingers and gave an overwhelming sense of being in the presence of more than an ordinary nun.

There have been times in my life when I have experienced an undeniable certainty that is inexpressible, and for lack of a more comprehensive term I have come to call that feeling faith. At that moment I was filled with it. Some use the word saint while others prefer enlightened. Not feeling either of them to be sufficient I will say I had an awareness of a physical sensation that this was the most spiritually evolved person I had ever met.

I had visited holy hermits in a number of places around the world, some self-proclaimed, while others truly gave off an aura of sanctity, but all of them had been men. This lady patted the stone, and as I sat next to her she covered my hand with her own and I felt an energy enter my body I had not known nor could I describe it other than saying it was an all pervading sense of well-being.

Something beyond words came into me from her. We sat in silence for an undetermined time as I was lost in my own serenity, and when she finally lifted her hand from mine I knew instinctively it was time to leave. We had not spoken as there was no need. I had received more from this woman in those few minutes than I had gained in a lifetime of wandering, and if the reader needs more explanation than that, I am simply not a gifted enough writer to impart it in words. Some things simply cannot be expressed.

While I have no illusions of ever attaining her degree of spiritual enlightenment, there have been many troubled times in my life when this woman has returned to my thoughts at a needed moment and I know it was by design because time has not dimmed the feeling she gave me.

Perhaps there really are guardian angels, but I will not know for sure in this lifetime.

If they do exist I met mine in a cave in Cambodia.

James Michael Dorsey is an explorer, author, artist, photographer and lecturer who has traveled extensively in 44 countries. His principle interest is documenting remote cultures in Africa and Asia. He is an eight-time SOLAS category award winner for best travel writing from Travelers' Tales, and has written for Colliers, The Christian Science Monitor, Los Angeles Times, the BBC and United Airlines.

He is a correspondent for Camerapix International, the oldest publishing firm in Africa, and has also written for Natural History, Wend, Sea Kayaker, Perceptive Travel, The Seattle Times, Orlando Sentinel, Chicago Tribune, and Travelers' Tales book series, plus several in-flight magazines of African airlines. His first book is entitled, Tears, Fear and Adventure, and his work has appeared in five separate anthologies. His second book, "Vanishing Tales from Ancient Trails" will be published soon. For more, see Jamesdorsey.com

ALICE
Nepal

I met her in a second-hand bookstore in Thamel, the tourist area of Katmandu. Thamel was always buzzing, assaulting its passers-by with colors, smells, loud noises. I'd been in that store on various occasions, buying books other people had read, leafing through the pages of well-traveled novels. Soaked in the smell of old paper, I felt safe and grounded, seeing glimpses of myself reflected in the words of others.

I'd traveled to Nepal to research women's rites and rituals, to write a story, make a film, be an artist — or so I thought. But, in truth, this was a way for me to avoid dealing with something that was still red and raw, that was bleeding me one drop at a time. I was desperately trying to let go of a relationship, which had left me exposed and scarred.

Although I'd been in Nepal for some months, I had no idea I was sick, I'd had no symptoms, until now. Malta fever. I'd contracted it in a village comprised of three families, one makeshift cheese factory and an abandoned Buddhist monastery, where I'd eaten some unpasteurized cheese. It had finally taken its toll on me. I'd become increasingly weak.

Unbearable headaches clouded my thinking and dulled my enjoyment of everything. Pain in my guts and diarrhea left me aching for days on end. It was in this condition, broken and confused, that I found Alice. Or she found me. Or we found each other. All I know is that's when she came into my life one hot, muggy day at the end of July, a day that clung around my neck, stifling me, making it hard to breathe.

She was sitting on the rough wooden floor, curled up with a book in the children's section. I don't remember what she was reading. I hardly noticed her, let alone the title of her book. My health and emotional state were all I could think about at the time.

At first I couldn't see her face, hidden behind her long, white-blonde hair, couldn't tell how young she was. All I knew was that she was a child, not a native, and alone in a second-hand foreign bookstore, reading on the floor.

I didn't pay her much attention. I looked through shelves of mixed-up titles, picked some out, put some back, read a page or two. I was in my own insular frame of mind, too self-involved to notice. I can't remember how we started talking. Maybe she smiled or asked me a question. I don't remember. But, that's not what mattered.

Soon I was sitting on the floor next to her, lost in the purity and clarity of her disarming blue eyes. She told me her name was Alice, and we discussed books.

"Oh, I read fantasy," she said. She was from Australia, and her accent sounded unfamiliar and twangy.

"Really? And what sort of fantasy do you prefer?"

"Anything I can get my hands on. But not adult stuff. Just for children."

"I see. And why's that?" I asked.

"Because that's where the magic happens," she replied, brushing her hair casually off her face.

I agreed. Growing up, I read a great deal. It allowed me to travel and be swept into worlds full of wondrous images and unfamiliar sensations. It unleashed my imagination. My hunger for anything unusual, my curiosity and love of what seemed impossible were satisfied in these stories. It's true. That *is* where the magic happened.

"Since you like stories," I said, "would you like me to show you one?"

Her eyes grew big, her freckles became more prominent. "Oh, yes, please!"

I took out a piece of paper from my bag and started folding it into various shapes: a square, a boat, a strange tree. By bending one flap down, a different image appeared, and with each form, a new story evolved. I am no origami expert, but my story must have been at least a little entertaining, because she put her book down, leaned on her crossed legs and turned to face me, staring at my fidgeting fingers.

"That's not a bear!" Alice said, her eyebrows gathered together.

"Oh," I said. "Well, maybe it isn't a bear. But a dog. A bear-eating dog, whose belly has grown so fat from having eaten the bear that it now looks like a mango!"

She squinted in concentration.

"What do *you* think it looks like?" I asked, handing her the creased paper.

"I don't know. Maybe a seal, or a whale."

"Hmm....perhaps a whale that's swallowed the bear-eating dog?"

Her laughter blasted through the bookstore, and a number of people peered at us from behind shelves.

"Don't be silly!" she said, and giggled behind her hand. She held the paper in her fingers, turned it this way and that, examining it, then placed it in her pocket.

"I'm hungry," I said, getting up to leave.

"So am I."

"Is your mother in the bookstore? Should we all go for lunch?"

Alice remained seated on the floor, her eyes cast down.

"She's not here."

"Ah, is she in another shop? Should we go find her?" I asked.

She shook her head.

"No. I won't see her today."

For a moment, I didn't know how to reply. I didn't have children of my own, yet, but my family was very close, and my mother would never have left any of us alone in a foreign city.

"What do you mean you're not going to see her today?" I asked. "Is your father with you?"

"He's not here. I don't know where he is."

I sat down again. Suddenly, I didn't feel that hungry anymore.

"So, who's taking care of you? Are you all alone?"

"No," she said, her voice light, still not raising her eyes. "My brother is with me."

Relief flowed through me. Her older brother was somewhere close by.

"Shall we find him, then? Is he in here?"

Again, she shook her head.

"No. He's in another shop."

"Well, let's go," I said, and made an attempt to move.

"He's 6."

"Six what?"

"Six years old."

Silence descended on us immediately. The book-covered walls of the store drew closer together.

"How old are you, Alice?" I asked, fearing the answer.

"I'm 9."

My throat dried up. I could hear my heartbeat in my ears.

"Nine? And...you're all alone?"

She shrugged her shoulders. Her fringe slipped in front of her face.

"And where's your mother?"

"In a place, with other people."

"What other people?"

"They sing and pray all day. It's boring there."

I rubbed my forehead. The heat crawled under my skin, seeping in my veins.

"Well...when will she come and get you and your brother?"

"She can't leave for another week," she replied, and flicked through the pages of the book she was holding.

I don't know what I was expecting to hear, but it was not this. I had no idea what to say or do.

"How long has she been there for?" I asked.

"I don't know. Three, four days."

"And what have you been doing all this time? Is there really no one else to look after you? Where exactly is your brother now, and why is he not with you?"

I was attacking her, I knew that. But the questions wouldn't stop coming. They flew out of my mouth before I'd even had a chance to filter them or spell them out to myself.

She remained silent for what seemed like a long time.

I heard someone clearing their throat and turned to look. The owner of the store stood above us, eyebrows raised in way of an apology.

"I'm sorry, but either you buy a book, or you have to go." He smiled, and I noticed one gold tooth.

"Yes, you're right," I said, standing up. I glanced at the book in my hands. "I'll buy this." It was *The Black Madonna*, a collection of short stories by Doris Lessing.

"Ah, excellent!" The man took the book from my hands and made his way to the cash register.

I was about to follow him, but stopped. Turning toward Alice, I bent down and held out my hand.

"Come," I said. She looked up at me with an almost blank expression in her face. "Let's go have some lunch."

She placed her hand in mine. It was cold in this suffocating humidity.

Lunch was a quiet affair. I took her to Bluebell vegetarian restaurant, a discovery I'd made on one of my first nights in Katmandu. The mushroom and spinach burger was unrivaled, and I returned there religiously. We sat opposite each other at a table next to the window, watching people in vibrantly-colored clothes walk by. At least, I did. She simply sipped her iced lemonade, bit into her veggie burger, nibbled on her fries. I ate, all the while stealing glances at her. She was so involved with her food, I didn't want to disturb her, and I didn't know when she'd last had a proper meal. My questions had made her clam up, yet I sensed that she wanted my company. She needed it.

Alice ate another burger, and then a pie, asking for a dollop of whipped cream on top. I ordered some tea, specifying that I wanted it without sugar or milk; the Nepalese idea of tea — milk, tea leaves and about a kilo of sugar — was not my idea at all. Our meal over, I paid and we left. Hardly a word had passed between us.

We walked around the streets of Thamel and beyond, to Durbar Square. I talked about the brown brick temples, the intricately carved wooden shutters and panels, the statue of Hanuman, the monkey god, covered with layers of red and gold fabric, looking more like a nondescript blob than a monkey.

I found a fruit stall and bought us a freshly squeezed orange juice, a twist of black pepper ground on top. We climbed the steps of the central temple, watched the multi-colored *tuk-tuks* and rickshaws as they hurried by, crammed to the brink with people, goats and chickens. And still not a single word from Alice.

"I think we'd best be heading back," I said, noticing the mellowing oranges and ultramarine blues in the sky. She nodded.

The need to be by myself suddenly overwhelmed me. Eating, walking, sitting together, feeling an immense sense of responsibility for this little stranger, yet not hearing her voice unnerved me. I wanted to get back to my hostel, undress and wash the sticky monsoon heat off my body. "I'll walk you to your hotel."

We reached the bookstore where we'd met, side by silent side.

"I'll stop here," she said.

I stared at her.

"Don't you have a place to stay?"

"I do, but I don't want to go there, yet."

I glanced at the sky, now an inky mauve. The glow of the gas lamps cast chiaroscuro shadows on our faces, the way they did in the Renaissance paintings I'd studied in art college.

"What will you do?" I asked.

"I'll read some books and wait for my brother," she said, waving her hand dismissively, one frail, gentle gesture that was quickly swallowed by the darkness.

"But, I can't leave you here. It's late." An oppressive feeling crept into my stomach.

"I'll be safe. Don't worry," she said, flashing me a weak smile.

"But..."

"Can we spend tomorrow together?"

"Yes, of course," I replied, unwilling to let her go. "But..."

"Bye," she said, disappearing behind stacks of books.

I remained motionless outside the store for some time, then, seeing that she wasn't coming out again, I walked away, headed toward my run-down hostel with its stone floor and cheap rates. I climbed the three flights of stairs to my room and collapsed on my bed fully dressed. Exhausted, I closed my eyes, turned onto my side and quickly fell asleep.

*****

Next morning found me just as tired as the previous night. No matter how much I rested, my joints ached, my limbs were frail. Weeks later, when I discovered what was wrong with me, I began to understand this debilitating and frustrating tiredness, but at the time I attributed it to the heat, the humidity and my crumbling emotions. I washed, got dressed, and went to the Pumpernickel Bakery for breakfast. I placed a bagel, plain tea and a small bowl of peanut butter on my tray, and walked out into the garden in the back, where green plants and a straw awning offered some shade.

I sat with my friends, an English girl named Emma, her sister Janice, my friend Jhangjup and two Tibetan men, "The Two Tenzings" as I called them. They were people I spent a fair amount of time with, but have since lost contact, a hazard I grew to recognize the more I traveled.

So many people appeared and disappeared, from all walks of life, and more countries than I can remember. We shared moments of laughter, became close, then drifted apart, like waves meeting at the shoreline. I grew to appreciate these meetings for what they were: a foreign place made less alien, the world made smaller, recognizable, a safe haven in an expansive, oftentimes harsh world. I needed to believe this.

I was deep in conversation with one of the sisters, when I felt a tap on my shoulder.

"Hi," Alice said, a fresh smile on her lips.

"Oh, hi," I replied. I had completely forgotten about her.

I pulled out the chair beside me and she plopped in it, throwing a small scruffy bag on the table. I introduced her to my friends and got her some breakfast.

"Where's your brother?" I asked, and she shrugged her shoulders.

"Around here somewhere."

"You should have brought him with you," I said, but regretted it immediately as she crossed her arms in front of her chest and looked sullen. I didn't pursue the matter, although it burned in my mind.

I asked how she knew where to find me, and she told me it hadn't been that difficult — all travelers go to the Pumpernickel Bakery for breakfast. I smiled at her ingenuity then resumed the conversation with my friends, discussing and comparing notes on different foods we'd tasted, places we'd visited and people we'd met.

"Are you staying in Katmandu long?" Alice asked.

Her question surprised me. I told her I would be leaving the day after tomorrow.

She made no response, but I could tell my answer troubled her.

"Since I won't be here much longer," I said, "shall we go on a little outing?"

Her smile was broad, immediate. Jhangjup said he'd join us.

"Where shall we go?" I asked.

"Well, that's easy," Jhangjup said. "Let's go to a safari park I know. It's a little out of the way, but it might be fun."

Alice jumped to her feet, clapping her hands. We said goodbye to the sisters and "The Two Tenzings," and together we set off for a day-trip outside Katmandu, near the town of Boudhanath, to the half-deserted safari park my friend knew. I worried that Alice's mother would be concerned about her and wonder where she was. But I could get nothing out of Alice, so I had to worry alone.

We clambered into a taxi. The driver sang to the radio music and occasionally spat burnt-red tobacco out the window. Conversation flowed easily. Alice sat between Jhangjup and me, holding both our hands. I closed my fingers round hers and felt the sweat gathering between our palms.

After an hour's drive, the taxi came to a halt, and we got out, still connected to each other.

Dark green vegetation and birds' calls greeted us. In the distance, we saw a forest of giant lofty *shala* trees, feathery mimosas displaying their yellow blossoms, and numerous silky oak, maple and firs wrapped with vines. The grounds were protected by the presence of the faraway Himalayan Mountains. I prayed we wouldn't get bitten by any snakes as we marched through tall grasses, but there was nowhere else to walk — this safari park was truly deserted and wild. Despite the increased humidity, I found myself forgetting about everything that had clung to me until now, no pains, no wounds to heal, only a lush expanse of land ahead beckoning us into its depths.

We reached a forest, and heard leaves and twigs crunch and break beneath our tread.

"Look there," Jhangjup said, pointing through the trees to an enclosed grassland on our right.

Alice covered her mouth with her hand in an attempt to suppress her squeal of excitement. Deer. A herd of chital deer, walking casually between trees, unhurried, so close and yet keeping their distance. Their pinkish taupe coats speckled with white dots and white underbelly stood out against the evergreens. They could see us and we could see them, but we did not disrupt their midday walk. They nibbled on *shala* leaves and casually sauntered off again on their long graceful legs.

"Did you see how *many* of them there were?" Alice said, her little shoulders shaking with exhilaration.

We walked farther into the untamed forest, found a small clearing with a little river running through it, and sat down to have our picnic of Danish pastries, pretzels and bottled water. I hadn't realized how hungry I was until we ate. Jhangjup and Alice told each other jokes. Alice had a few bites, then decided it would be more fun to take off her shoes and splash around in the river.

"No, wait," I cried, afraid of how deep it might be and whether there were sharp or slippery rocks. I ran after her and caught up as she was stepping into the water.

"It's great!" she said. "Come in!"

Although I had no desire to join her, I took off my shoes and socks and stepped into the river. It was, indeed, cool. No slimy surfaces or jutting edges. The running water refreshed me. Jhangjup joined us, and he and Alice started splashing each other. We were all soaked through before I could climb out and run back to our picnic spot, laughing.

I sat on the flattened grass, ready to dry my feet, when I noticed strange worm-like creatures on them, so dark they were almost black.

"What *are* they?" I said, trying to sweep them off my toes.

Jhangjup knelt by me.

"They're leeches. Don't try to pull them off."

"Leeches!" I cried.

"Here, sit still," he said, taking out a lighter and a pack of cigarettes from his trouser pocket. He lit one up.

"Now, don't move. I will try to smoke them off, but if you're not still, I might burn you," he said, taking hold of my feet.

I nodded.

The de-leeching process took longer than I expected and I was amazed at how those little bloodsuckers refused to detach themselves, how they stubbornly clung on. I watched as Jhangjup held the cigarette next to their squirming black bodies. They lifted one side off first, then peeling backward like a curly wooden shaving, dropped off my feet one by one.

I thanked Jangjup and stared at the red sores on my skin.

"It might take about a week for those bites to disappear," he said, "but, don't worry, they're not infected."

My feet covered once more, I sat back, watched Alice as she bounced around us, chasing white butterflies that had appeared out of nowhere.

"I'm worried about her," I said.

Jhangjup turned to look at me. "Why?"

"She's all alone, her mother's off in an ashram or a monastery, from what I can gather, and her younger brother is wondering around Katmandu on his own."

My friend studied Alice for a few minutes.

"Don't worry," Jhangjup said.

"How can you say that?"

"Because she has good survival skills."

"What do you mean?" I asked.

"I think she instinctively knows who to trust, enjoys every moment, yet lets go of it easily. Maybe this will change when she's older, and she might either become overly attached to people or unable to connect to them. I don't know. Anything's possible. But, right now...look at her."

Her carefree prancing showed me nothing else existed for Alice. No worries clouded her joy. Pure, innocent, untamed childhood. Jhangjup was right — it probably wouldn't last. She'd grow up, clutter her mind and become aware of the missing pieces in her life, as happened to every adult. It was unavoidable. Still, I envied the ease with which she accepted whatever came her way without judging or asking questions.

"This is the best day *ever*!" Alice said, running toward us.

"Really? In what way?" I asked.

"Are you joking?" she exclaimed. "A picnic, deer...leeches? How can it get better than *that*?"

I smiled. Jhangjup glanced at his watch.

"It's getting late. We'd better go." We all agreed, gathered our stuff, and started walking back in the direction we'd come with Alice skipping ahead of us.

The late-afternoon sky was beginning to turn a rich orange-yellow, tinged with ribbons of lavender. Small noises tickled our ears, insects flitted and unseen animals scurried in the thickets.

"What was that?" Alice said all of a sudden, her voice a little above a whisper. "Did you hear it?"

We stopped in our tracks, extended our necks, hardly dared to breathe. I must admit, I heard nothing. I looked at Jhangjup and he placed his finger over his lips, warning us not to speak.

And then it came, a heavy footfall, slow, steady, getting louder as it approached. Alice took a step in my direction, grabbed hold of my hand, squeezed it so tight I thought the blood would stop pumping. The sound seemed to be coming from various directions; it was up high among the tallest branches, as well as on the ground.

A man's voice, one long drawn-out note ascending in pitch, bounced off the trees. My heart raced. It came again, his call, and then a thumping sound, getting closer and closer. Alice moved slowly behind me, still holding my hand.

That's when we saw it. An elephant. A massive, breathtaking beast of an animal, so large we had to bend our heads back to see the man sitting on top, balancing his weight, holding onto nothing at all. We stood paralyzed, and simply watched as it ambled before us, swaying its hips and trunk, the ground shaking with each thudding footstep. Its only acknowledgement of us was a flap of its ears.

I felt Alice push against my back, nudge me closer to the elephant. Without thinking, I reached out, brushed my fingertips across its tough grey skin, held my breath as its energy and strength jolted through my body, electrifying it. This was life! And I was living it again, thanks to Alice's gentle push.

The man on its back raised his arm in greeting, and continued on. Alice ventured a few steps away from me, following in the elephant's direction.

We stood still long after it had gone, unable or unwilling to move. Darkness started descending around us. We hurried to the exit.

We reached the road, now quite desolate and streaked with plentiful shadows, then walked for about another hour to the nearby town of Boudhanath. Exhausted, we hailed a taxi and drove back to Katmandu.

"I've never seen a *real* elephant, only photos in books," Alice said as we were nearing Thamel. "I'll never forget this day."

I smiled and placed a kiss on the top of her head.

The taxi reached my hostel and we all got out. Jhangjup wished us both good night and left, saying he'd meet us tomorrow at the Pumpernickel Bakery for breakfast. I walked Alice back to the bookstore. She turned and entered. I stood staring after her, oblivious to everything around me, until the cry of a rickshaw driver brought me back to the present.

"Watch out!" he cried. I turned around and went on my way.

Annia Lekka was born in Thessaloniki, Greece. She has a BA degree in theater design from Central Saint Martin's College of Art and Design, London, and a MA degree in creative writing from Lancaster University. She received a scholarship from the Royal West of England Academy for research studies in Nepal. She worked as a set and costume designer in Athens and London, and a stage manager at the Athens Concert Hall. She has three published novels and is working on her fourth novel. She lives in Athens with her music composer/sound engineer husband and their three children.

THE INDELIBLE DANIÈLE
France

When I first approach the 500-year-old farm, I'm not sure I've come to the right place. The address Danièle Mazet-Delpeuch had given me a month earlier when I called her for an interview was simply "La Borderie," the name of her French home and cooking school sewn into the fringes of a diminutive village in the rolling hills of the Dordogne, a region of southwestern France also known as Périgord. It is noted for its rustic regional specialties, such as duck, black truffles and foie gras, and a culinary pedigree steeped, quite literally, in goose fat.

Only a hand-painted wooden sign nailed to a tree points the way off the main road toward a cluster of unembellished stone and pitch-roofed cottages down a gravel drive, the simplicity of which catches me off guard. Maybe it is the flamboyance of TV star chefs that has tainted my imagination, but I expect more flash from the home of Danièle Mazet-Delpeuch, a name that attracts superlatives in this part of France. "Famous" and "a local legend," people had said when I told them I was going to meet the woman who'd not only started the region's first cooking school, but had also been hand-plucked from her simple surroundings to spend two years at the presidential palace in Paris as the personal chef of François Mitterrand, then president of France.

"We are not going to talk about that now," she says when I jump to questions a little too soon for her liking.

There is something delicate about Danièle, but she's far from frail. Her silver hair is smoothed into a bun pinned at the back of her head, revealing silky ivory skin that belies her age, which I don't dare ask. In a black collarless Chinese-style jacket worn over loose pants, she glides with fluid precision around the main room of the house, which is divided in two by a giant, double-sided fireplace, the kitchen and a seating area on one side, the dining table and sliding door to a scruffy garden on the other. It could be the set of a French movie.

Dainty, scallop-edged lace curtains cover petite square windows, and straw hats and baskets hang from sturdy wood beams that stretch across the ceiling. On the kitchen half of the room where I stand, a lamp with a glass tulip-shaped shade glows atop a spindly-legged table on which two scrapbooks bulge. I finger the cover of one of them and flip through the pages stuffed with photos, name tags, ribbons, menus and other markers of time's passage. I stop at a photo of her with the former

French president and Danièle sees me reading the accompanying yellowed newspaper article.

"I suppose I will always be remembered as that, more than anything else I have done," she says.

The concession in her voice stops me from shelling her with more questions. I close the scrapbook and sit down in a plump chair to watch her flit between the narrow, tile-top counters in her kitchen where she's finessing a paring knife that rhythmically slices *sanglier* (wild boar) into even pieces, to the fireplace where her arms pinwheel and arc as she rhapsodizes about the joy of preparing a meal.

"Cooking is so much more than just eating," she says. "It is talking and being social, and making people as happy as you can with the food you prepare. You are putting on a *spectacle*."

Danièle speaks English, but peppers her sentences with words in her native French. She also talks with her hands and whatever is in them. The house, she tells me, waving a fireplace poker like a magic wand, is where her father was born, where her four children were raised, and where she welcomes them and her six grandchildren each summer.

Thirty years earlier, Danièle began Foie Gras Weekends at the house, a three-day course teaching the regional Périgord cuisine, and four years after that, founded the *École d'Art et Tradition Culinaire du Périgord*, the region's first cooking school. These endeavors earned her a formidable reputation and several awards, including the *Chevalier du Mérite Agricole* from the French agricultural industry, an award rarely bestowed upon a woman.

Danièle stokes the coals of the fire again and flecks of orange flee up the chimney like fireflies.

As an author researching the food, cooking traditions and local personalities of the region for a culinary travel book, I would be careless not to include Danièle in my writing, which is why I've come. But truthfully, I would have probably come anyway. I've been a lifelong Francophile, drawn for unexplained reasons to a culture, a language and a country that I have no ancestral ties to, yet where I feel most at home. I took French in high school, and was a French major in college. I remember being asked by one of my teachers what I wanted to be when I grew up, and I said, "an ambassador to France." After becoming a journalist, it was my goal to write about travel, and in particular about France, a country I have loved, unconditionally, since I first taped a picture of the Eiffel Tower to my bedroom wall as a child. In a way, I now considered myself an ambassador, bringing genuine curiosity with me when I traveled to France, and typing up slices of French culture and life for my compatriots in America.

After a few minutes, Danièle breaks my reverie. "You know," she says, "I live almost like my grandmother did."

The house indeed appears time-capsuled, and Danièle confirms that not much has changed over the generations, except for the addition of refrigeration and plumbing. The room is full but tidy, and includes the kitchen and dining and living room, where a sliding door leads to the garden. But the *pièce de résistance* is that enormous fireplace, which opens on two sides, at least 5 feet wide, to the kitchen and the dining area. It is the home's obvious epicenter, and Danièle tells me she designed it herself with entertaining in mind. A slew of archaic tools leans against the brick façade, and varied pots wait to nest in the gray and glowing ashes. Danièle picks up a black cast iron pan called a *royale* and sets it down in the embers. She tells me it's more than a century old.

"The trick is, you never wash them," she says, wiping the inside with a cloth. When I ask her what she cooks in the *royale*, she says, "Everything — a whole turkey, a *lièvre* (wild hare), a cake."

With that she takes a paintbrush, dips it in a nearby can of goose fat and coats the inside of the *royale*. Within minutes the scent of the Dordogne's favorite cooking elixir suffuses the room. She snuggles six meaty duck legs into place on top of the bubbling fat, and caps them with a lid. The fireplace is large enough to stand upright in. I ask if she ever hangs geese or lamb from the brawny hooks dangling from the dark void of the chimney.

"No, that's cooking for tourists," she laughs.

Watching Danièle, I imagine the generations of instruction, decisions, arguments and revelations that have transpired around her hearth, and I picture her family and friends celebrating birthdays, graduations and holidays, with old friends and new, gathered around this stone fireplace that's both an intersection in her house and her life.

As a child growing up in Los Angeles, I wasn't accustomed to fireplaces at all, let alone meals prepared over burning wood in the center of the living room. Meals were merely sustenance for my mom, a single, independent woman of the '70s who felt cooking was not necessarily about entertaining or even pleasing, but about convenience. Vegetables from a can, pasta from a box and fried chicken from the freezer that could be heated in the oven or microwave. They were easy, cheap meals and almost always served on paper plates. The kitchen wasn't the hub of our family or social life, and I never imagined it could be.

As I started to travel to France, I discovered that dining is the country's social glue. Days are planned around meals, shops close from noon to 2pm for lunch, and cooking is often the best glimpse into family histories, where recipes are passed on as cherished heirlooms, like old photos and wedding china. It was easy to envision my own home someday, where I would host long family dinners and cook meals from recipes that I'd pass on to my daughter. It wasn't until I got older and began to cook in my own kitchen that I understood the joy that comes from inviting people you care about into your home, and demonstrating that emotion through a lovingly prepared meal.

I'm not surprised when Daniele tells me she wel-comes friends, family, journalists and tourists a few times a week to her home and table. Today, she is ex-pecting a radio show host from Santa Rosa, CA, and his wife, and has also invited friends who own a nearby bed and breakfast. She busily prepares lunch for them but still makes time to offer me coffee in a porcelain floral teacup. While I sip, she whisks into the garden to pluck a handful of figs from the tree, which she plans to pair with the *sang&ier* for a savory-sweet *amuse-bouche*. She invites me to stay, but the polite American in me de-clines, telling her I don't want to impose, and apologizing for having come at such a hectic time. She looks at me inquisitively.

"You know if you make an appointment for 11 in the morning here in the Périgord, it is expected you will have something to eat," Daniele says, pointing at me with the knife she is now using to slice the figs. "I planned for you to stay."

She explains that this courteous custom stems from times when people would travel four to five days by horse and carriage. Even though I've come only two hours by car, I accept her invitation.

With the pleased nod of someone who is used to get-ting her way, Daniele scoops up a dish of potatoes from her counter top and excuses herself to warm them in the oven, located in the demonstration kitchen next door. While she's gone, I look around the room more closely, mostly to verify there really is no oven, and Danièle is revealed in pieces.

Antique curios dot the ochre-colored stone walls, as do photos of smiling apron-clad guests standing arm-in-arm with Danièle. Oval frames line bookcases and shelves, and ring gap-toothed grins of children sitting on her lap, or posed in white-collar school uniforms. On a wooden buffet underneath the lace-covered windows, dozens of jars of homemade *confiture* stack like building blocks next to glass domes preserving frosted cakes and flaky fruit pies, each with a few missing wedges. Her life might be simple, but it is certainly not empty.

I again fumble through the pages of one of her scrapbooks. Danièle's gastronomic life is formidable and has taken her around the world as a lecturer, teacher and chef, and to places as diverse as China, Mexico, New York, Montreal, Moscow and Sydney. She even spent 14 months in Antarctica, where she cooked at a French research lab, rang in the millennium and fêted her 60th birthday. When she returns, I ask her about that.

"I was looking for a change — an adventure," she says, signaling me to follow her.

She pulls jewel-toned apéritif glasses from a cabinet near the dining table and hands them to me two at a time. I set them down on the faded blue tablecloth next to round ceramic plates that, despite the summer season, are embellished with an autumn leaf motif. From a chunky wooden chest of deep drawers she grabs water goblets and wine glasses, and we tweak them into their proper positions on the table. She counts out cutlery from yet another drawer and places it, piece by piece, upon each blue cloth napkin.

"This is the French way," she says, holding up a fork until my eyes lock onto it. "The tines go down so that guests can see the family crest on the back of the silverware."

There is no crest on the back of any of her stainless steel forks, and I ask if she always goes to such lengths when setting the table, using three different sets of glasses, cloth napkins and tine-down fork placement for a mid-week lunch.

"But, of course. It is the very least I can do for my guests."

Part of what lures me to France year after year, and has since my first visit as a young adult, is the country's collective love affair with food and the perfected art of the long and lingering meal, an experience that can be as aesthetic and sensually stimulating as the masterpieces hanging in the Louvre or the sopranos on stage at the Opera House.

As Danièle slowly circles the table, carefully placing the forks in their rightful setting, she comments on a brightly colored portrait of an almost cartoonish-looking woman I am admiring. She points a fork in my direction. She tells me Monique Peytral, the local artist who painted the facsimile of the Lascaux Cave, the Dordogne's most-visited site, painted it. The original Lascaux Cave, featuring 17,000-year-old drawings by

Cro-Magnon man, was closed to the public in 1963. Monique Peytral worked on a replica from 1972 to 1983, when Lascaux II, as the new site is called, opened.

"She is a very good friend of mine and was just here for dinner the other night," Danièle says.

It seems fitting that this painting watches over the table, and I love the idea of these two artists and preservers of local history sitting down together to enjoy and admire one another's craft.

Back at the fire, the duck legs sizzle in the *royale,* and Danièle turns them in their bubbling bed. In an elegant *pas de deux,* platters of pâté and figs stuffed with *sanglier* arrive on the table just as her guests knock on the door. Danièle makes a round of introductions, kissing cheeks and squeezing hands. She pours a traditional and homemade *vin de noix* (walnut wine) into the apéritif glasses we'd set out earlier, and raises hers into the air. "*Bienvenue,* old friends and new."

There are eight of us around Danièle's table; a coterie of curious French and English speakers, some here for the first time, others returning to the table of a woman whose generosity and passion for her region's culinary history is cooked into every bite.

After the *amuse-bouche* of sweet figs and salty *sanglier* comes an appetizer of *foie gras* with fig jam. The *confit de canard* (duck legs) that had been simmering in the *royale* arrive on our plates next. The skin is crisped and browned to a caramel color, and juice streams from the inside when I pierce it with my knife. This dish is found in homes and on menus everywhere in the Dordogne. It's their version of what we'd call comfort food, and is prepared in the traditional way by frying in its own fat, something Danièle tells me she remembers her grandmother teaching her how to do. The duck is served alongside the potatoes she'd warmed up earlier. They are the most heavenly spuds I've ever tasted, golden and crunchy on the outside, and soft to the bite, cooked the night before, Danièle tells us in, what else, goose fat.

As is often the case in France, the meal includes a cheese course, then dessert, followed by coffee, and stretches through several bottles of wine and well into twilight. Our voices ping-pong around the table, and scatter between bouts of laughter and stomach-rubbing stretches of silence. We share stories about our hometowns and favorite restaurants; recap books we've read and which movies and music made us laugh and cry; brag about where we've traveled and where we're going; reminisce about our loved ones and children back home; and of course wax lyrical about the Dordogne and Danièle.

Over the course of an afternoon, our motley cohort transforms from being just a group of strangers at a table into a temporary family, connected, if only for an ephemeral moment, by our host, the table and, of course, the food, which as expected, is delicious. But it's not the food I savor the most.

The essential ingredient baked into this memorable meal is that intangible human communion we seek when we travel. It is a bond fortified, I believe, when like-minded spirits come together with open minds and hearts, and open themselves to others around the table, as is so often the case in France.

After the last visitor leaves, I linger intentionally, and offer to help clean up. Danièle declines my offer and makes one of her own. "Now that you've spent time in my home and we've gotten to know one another a little, I am ready to answer your questions."

Danièle had mentioned earlier that she is likely to be remembered as the ex-cook of an ex-president of France, but by now I have almost forgotten about that part of her life because I discovered she is so much more. She is a mother, a grandmother, a teacher, an explorer, a friend, a historian, and adventurer, and a gracious, albeit fork-wielding, hostess.

But mostly I realize she is an artist who re-creates her greatest opus over and over again — that innate flair for making people feel good just by being present, and feel at home, even when they are oceans from their own — all dished out with a genuine passion for her homeland that is reciprocated in equal measure.

I do have a few more questions for Danièle, about her family; her cooking school; her friends; her beloved Périgord and its cuisine; and her thoughts about being considered a gastronomic rock star. But I tell her the questions can wait a bit, and that I'd really just like to enjoy her company and her table a little longer.

She nods, satisfied, it seems, that the lesson has been taught and learned, and we share one more glass of wine by the fire.

Kimberley Lovato is a freelance writer whose work has appeared in print and online media including National Geographic, AFAR, American Way, Delta Sky, Virginia Living, Marin Magazine, travelandleisure.com, bbc.com, frommers.com and lonelyplanet.com. Her essays have won awards and been anthologized in Best Women's Travel Writing, while her book, Walnut Wine & Truffle Groves, received the Gold 2012 Lowell Thomas Award from the Society of American Travel Writers Foundation. www.kimberleylovato.com

WHITE NIGHTS
Finland

Two steps down the Finnair ramp onto the tarmac at the Helsinki Airport and I knew I had made a mistake wearing cowboy boots. The frozen ground shot an almost electric jolt up through my heels to my calves. A third step landed me backside down on the ice-coated passenger walkway. What was I doing in Helsinki, Finland (61°15'N and 28°15'E), not far from the Arctic Circle in late January when the temperature falls below zero degrees F and daylight is a drizzle of illumination from 9:30 to 3:30?

I had come to this most remote of Scandinavian countries looking for a cold-weather adventure. The impetus: I'd read the previous September about Sir Ernest Shackleton's ill-fated attempt to reach the South Pole in 1914. His ship became trapped in the ice, forcing him and his expedition to trek through the endless whitescape for months and then row 800 miles to safety at an out-post at the edge of civilization. That men could prevail over such dreadful hardships, living on little more than seal blubber, seems almost unimaginable, especially as I happened to be reading the volume with my back against a beachfront wall in 80-degree weather south of Los Angeles.

I am a native Californian who grew up splitting time between the Pacific Ocean and the high desert. I'm usually in deck shoes or Western boots. I know how to sail a boat, and I know how to ride a horse. But the only snow I know is out a car window on the occasional mountain trip.

And that's why I was wearing cowboy boots when I came off the plane in Helsinki, having opted for the edge of the Arctic rather than the Antarctic for a cold-weather experience, suspecting that reindeer steaks in a city are preferable to seal blubber on an ice floe.

Outside the airport I caught a cab to my hotel, showered and changed into waffle-stomper boots and newly purchased subzero clothes — like much of humankind I get the L.L. Bean catalog — that made me feel as padded out as the Michelin Tires mascot. Then I went out about 7:30 p.m. for a walk in the dark on the main thoroughfare, Mannerheim Boulevard.

I was exhausted from the all-night flight, kept awake by two large women, apparently sisters, in the row behind me who had filled most of 12 hours talking about miracles while eating M&Ms from a bag large enough to qualify as additional luggage.

Despite Helsinki's falling snow and glacial temperature, cars filled Mannerheim, while a line of people waited patiently to enter a nearby Cineplex and mobs of customers were going in and out of Stockman's, the leading department store. These Finns seemed oblivious to the horrific cold: Just a hardy lot of people with tingling faces and red cheeks and the occasional wet nose. The Finnish women, with high cheekbones, seemed especially beautiful, many in fur coats, the sort that would enrage PETA members in the U.S. But in this climate there is at least a weather justification.

The hotel concierge, on the way out, warned me not to walk too close to buildings because stalactites of ice hanging down from roofs often become too heavy and crash like enormous daggers on the unsuspecting.

Two blocks from the hotel I found a shop selling heated wraps of meat, though not reindeer, and vegetables bundled in pastry shells. I had two and a dessert made with cloudberries, a remarkable fruit that somehow grows in the arctic tundra and looks something like raspberries but with a sweeter taste.

I went back to my room and found myself too tired, too jetlagged, too time-zone-shifted just to sleep. So I tuned the television in to a strange film about gentlemen wrestlers in the late 1800s that seemed to be in Swedish. I drifted in and out of consciousness several times and didn't crawl back to life until a morning rerun of "The Muppets" roused me

After a shower, I looked out my window into the pitch-black morning to see office workers arriving at a building across the way and one woman on the sixth floor nursing a plant that had a long way to go until the continuous northern light of summer arrived.

My plan for the next two days was to visit the Helsinki seaport with its giant Baltic icebreaker ships and to walk the city's streets, taking in the museums and monuments. I also wanted to shop for gifts to please my wife who tends to put on the central heat when the temperature drops below 70 degrees in southern California. I figured to warm myself up as needed in the cafés that line Helsinki's streets.

I also wanted to find my way to the central train station to see about visiting Turku, the oldest Finnish city that dates to the 13th century and served as its capital until the Russians took Finland away from Swedes in the early-1800s. I imagined a train slicing through an infinite expanse of snow like a scene from "Doctor Zhivago."

But then I met Aki in the Digelius music shop. A Finn in his 40s, he was looking at a rare Sir Douglas Quintet album on the Swedish Sonet label that never had an American release. The SDQ had been a major American act during the late-1960s and early-1970s, scoring hits with "She's About a Mover" and "Mendocino," and then improbably became the toast of Scandinavia after its U.S. fame waned. Later, in the 1990s, the key members changed the band's name to the Texas Tornados and, with the addition of Freddy Fender and Flaco Jimenez, became hit-makers in the U.S. again.

I mentioned to Aki that I'd once interviewed Doug Sahm — Sir Douglas himself — for a magazine piece, and that was enough. Aki and I were still talking hours later, and I became a dinner guest for a Karelian stew of lamb with vegetables and peppercorns that his wife Inge prepared that night.

Aki's family, he told me, lived in the Karelian region of Finland until the Soviet Union, fresh from carving up Poland with its then ally Germany in 1939, decided it wanted the Karelian Isthmus also and launched what the Finns call the Winter War (1939-1940). The Finnish Army, wearing white parkas and fighting on skis, waged an uneven battle against the massed Soviet forces before sheer numbers forced capitulation, causing most of Karelia to be lost to the Soviets. Finland's population at the time was 3.7 million, while the neighboring USSR numbered 200 million. But the Finns managed several victories, including the destruction of a large armored tank force and supporting infantry that they lured onto an ice-covered river and then bombarded with artillery fire, sending machines and men to the icy bottom.

"We took back most of the Karelia in the Continuation War [1941-1944] when we attacked the Russians while they were busy fighting the Nazis. They got most of the land back, though. Those of us who were displaced still hate them."

Most Finns are fluent in Finnish and Swedish, the two official national languages, as well as English and German, but tend not to speak Russian even though as a next-door neighbor Russia is a major trading partner. "We still laugh about when they tried to bomb our biggest hospital during the Continuation War, but blew up their own embassy instead."

Aki convinced me that I should abandon my plan to take the train to Turku the next day, saying that if old buildings were what I wanted to see there were many available much closer in Porvoo, a town dating to the mid-1300s just 50 kilometers from Helsinki. He offered to drive me there.

Inge added I should stay out of the train station anyway. "That's where the alcoholics will ask you for money and cigarettes. They are our real crime problem." She obviously has never been in an American train or bus station or visited the Port Authority building in New York City. Helsinki averages about 10 homicide and manslaughter cases a year, while New Orleans, for instance, with a roughly comparable population, had 193 in 2012, according to the New Orleans Police Department.

The next morning, which looked more like midnight than 8:30 a.m., Aki picked me up in a restored Nissan Cherry, a sister model to the Datsun 310 sold in the U.S. in the 1980s. His wife drives a new BMW, but he likes tinkering with old cars, this one having been found in a village barn where it had been stored for years from snow, storm and summer heat.

For a 30-year-old car, the Cherry handled the snow-blanketed roads well, keeping up with new Volvos (their unofficial motto being "They're boxy but they're safe"), various imports and the occasional weary Saab. Also there were heavy trucks on the road, many of them built by a Finnish company called Sisu, the word for guts, grit and determination. They looked Leviathan enough for that U.S. cable show called "Ice Road Truckers" on the History Channel.

Porvoo turned out to have two districts: The new town, which is exactly what it sounds like, and the old town with winding streets too narrow for many vehicles, including mechanized snow plows, and wooden houses that date back six and seven centuries. The center of Porvoo is a 15th century cathedral, with some parts dating to the 1300s, sacred to the Evangelical Lutheran Church. It is where the first Diet of Finland took place in 1809, establishing the region as the Grand Duchy of Finland under the Russian tsar.

Not far from the cathedral we found a snow-covered bakery with goods that made me feel embarrassed for being from the country that foisted Famous Amos, Mrs. Fields and Cinnabon on the world. Cloudberries in pastry shells may well be true manna of the Gods, Nordic division.

From Porvoo it was a short drive through the snow-fields to Haikko, a spa where the tsars went to take the healing waters. After the 1917 Russian revolution, when Finland broke away to establish its own independence, the remaining members of the Romanov family lived there for a time before scattering to avoid Bolshevik assassins.

The spa was closed that day for plumbing repairs, but Aki prevailed on one of the attendants to let me do a quick walk through. It was easy to image Nicholas II — Emperor of Russia, Grand Duke of Finland, King of Poland — and his family, including young Anastasia, wandering the dark-wooded rooms. All that was missing were mounted stag and boar heads and crossed swords on the walls. If you have ever watched "The Prisoner of Zenda" on the Turner Classic Movies channel, you will have a fair idea of the décor.

Outside on the snow-blanketed grounds, Aki convinced a Laplander hauling wood on a horse-drawn sleigh to give the visiting American a ride. I tried to beg off — being pulled in a sleigh seemed a little too Currier & Ives — but they insisted, and I ended up going for a 20-minute jaunt, the sleigh runners throwing snow as we went up and down hillocks and dodged trees. The Lap-landers are an ancient people who live in the Arctic region and were there long before the Stone Age ancestors of the Finnish people migrated from Central Europe. The Laps are the nomads of the north, kindred spirits to Native Americans and the Ainu people of Japan.

That night back in Helsinki, I took Aki and Inge out to dinner, going of all places to a Russian restaurant. "We're not fond of the Russians, but we like their food," Inge told me. Fortunately they picked a quiet place without dancing Cossacks. Having spent the previous days in the waffle-stompers, I'd switched back to my cowboy boots. Aki offered to put old tire treads on their bottoms, but I declined.

I spent the rest of my time in Helsinki prowling the National Museum of Finland, the Helsinki Design Museum, the City Art Museum, the Finnish Architecture Museum, Finlandia Hall, where President Ford and other heads of state in 1975 signed the Helsinki Accords easing tensions between Western and Eastern Blocs, and the monument to composer Jean Sibelius (1865-1957), whose music was outlawed by the Russians when they ruled over Finland and now provides the soundtrack for his nation.

I also managed to hike out two kilometers through the snow to the site of the 1952 Summer Olympics where a bronze statue of Paavo Nurmi, who set 22 world track records and earned nine gold and three silver Olympic medals, looked a trifle chilled as depicted mid-stride in his running shorts. I, on the other hand, had acclimated.

Then, my week in a cold, cold climate concluded, I headed to the airport where the waffle-stompers went back into the duffle bag. I was ready for deck shoes and sunshine.

Bill Wasserzieher writes about music, film and travel. His byline has appeared in publications ranging from the Village Voice and L.A. Weekly to Smithsonian Air & Space and Boeing Frontiers. Many of his articles are available via computer, including a selection of his music pieces at the Rock's Back Pages website (www.rocksbackpages.com).

CREDITS

ACKNOWLEDGMENTS

Thanks to former Denver Post Travel Editor Mim Swartz for your editing expertise and advice, and to the multi-talented Gina Kremer for your suggestions. It's a pleasure working with you both!

A special thanks to Fredrik Härén of Ideas Island for sharing your beautiful island cottage as I wrote and put the book together. As you've said, "People who give themselves plenty of time to reflect and rest are more successful in being creative." I agree completely.

Thanks most of all to Ben, Kirstin, Keri and Matthew. You are my favorite traveling companions — and wherever you are is the place that I will always call home.

CPSIA information can be obtained at www.ICGtesting.com
Printed in the USA
BVOW03s0750250215

389207BV00001B/39/P